Finding Me

By

Christopher Ross, B.S, M.S.L

Copyrights © 2023 Christopher Ross

All Rights Reserved

Contents

Dedication i

About the Author iii

Synopsis 1

Introduction 2

Chapter 1 Unleashing the God-Given Potential 4

Chapter 2 You Co-Own Your Destiny 8

Chapter 3 Value Your worth 19

Chapter 4 Know your Worth 27

Chapter 5 Re-Building your Worth 33

Chapter 6 Re-Identifying who you are 36

Chapter 7 Re-Strategize, Re-Verbalize, and Re-Mobilize 40

Chapter 8 Re-Invest Yourself 50

Chapter 9 Releasing Inadequacy 55

Chapter 10 Releasing Negative Energies 66

Chapter 11 The Winner in Me 71

Chapter 12 The Leading, The Lesson and the Learning 75

Chapter 13 Re-Construction 79

Chapter 14 Renewal of your Focus 87

Dedication

This book is dedicated to my father, Elder Earl B. Ross, Sr who is the inspiration for this book. Overcoming the loss of a son, he continues to persevere; serving as a leadership for the family as they were dealing with the untimely death of his namesake. He has taught me many things in my upbringing what it takes to survive in a world where society trics to place identities on you; encouraging you to live out the true meaning of who and whose you are. Having a COGIC ministry whose aim was to respect all people with God being the center, it was a place where everybody was somebody. This dedication aims to let him know that all of the skills and the messages given in being reared by him were not forgotten or ill received but capitalized on and remembered. He remains to be one of the most influential people in my life and will continue to be. As attributing this literary work to him, I encourage him to always and continue to be the model that he has been for young men for the rest of his life. To my father, Earl B. Ross, Sr. I say Thank you!!!!

About the Author

The author of Finding Me is Christopher Ross, who was born in Grand Rapids, MI, but now resides in Magnolia, MS. Having early built foundations in the Churches of God in Christ, Inc, he serves as a Minister of encouragement, positive affirmations, and Minister of the gospel in the Missionary Baptist reformation. He is the father of one daughter, Christian Shemaiah Ross, the greatest achievement of his life. He holds solace that nothing of this sort could have been done without a higher deity guiding and shaping his submitted yet humble life.

He holds a Bachelor of Arts degree in Political Science, a Bachelor of Science degree in Professional Studies from Jackson State University, a Master of Science degree in Leadership from Belhaven University, and is currently a candidate for Doctorate in Philosophy degree from Jackson State University. An alumnus (2015) of Mississippi Black Leadership Institute, the author pushes community-based initiatives as he has a passion for seeing communities thrive and not be left behind. Attaining an award signed by Senator Bennie G. Thompson in April 2015 for community service, he is holding onto the philosophical idea that communities thrive when education survives. He has served in several guidance capacities, the first of which happened in 2014, when he became the mentor for the McComb High School and South Pike School, he served as director for the Senior Transition program for Amite, North Pike, South Pike, and McComb High schools. From there, he went on to become the Director of the Pike County Department of Human Services, which served to be one of the greatest challenges of Stewart and Leadership of his life. Meeting the challenge, the call to help people find their purpose and God-given potential, the author remains dedicated to empowering, providing motivation and leadership strategies.

Ecclesiastically, the author has served as an Evangelism President in the COGIC reformation and continues to provide words of encouragement and comfort for people on their quest to find themselves.

His literary works include a S.W.O.T analysis of Jackson city in Mississippi and a published book entitled. The Fellowship: An Ecumenical Approach to Religion published in 2015. His passion is to always be a beacon of encouragement for young innovative minds who are in search of their true biblical identities.

Synopsis

This book is a documented account of the quests of individuals to find their God given calling and or potential. As its title suggests, Finding Me is the ability to identify and find your unique identity from the creator, the one who has created you and discover what He has created you for. The book aims to encourage it's readers to look into what God says about you and who you are and created to do, it chronicles this by telling stories, factual stories that the reader could find themselves in. Building on the fact that the best way to curtail mentalities is through education, the book aims to provide educational information as stated by God through prophets and followers to let readers know that other's have had to experience the same things that we do. The book allows the reader to know that the atmosphere that we choose to live in is created by our ability to believe in the promises of God. Knowing that His promises are yes and amen, it shows the reader that discovering the potential that is inside is not hard, when we line up with the word of God. As in the opening lines of the book, we are pre-disposed to certain unalienable rights and just like in the ecclesiastical area we are privy to those same rights, and once we take ownership of them, finding yourself will be very attainable. The book aims to serve as a conduit to connect the earthly thoughts of an individual to the supernatural thoughts of that individual; it aims to be an encouragement providing hope for its readers and that hope can only be found in the word of God. It suggests that we all go through a construction time in our lives, and that the construction time is the time where we are to trust God, trust His promises because it's certain that the construction will come to an end and we will be better for it and come out with our purpose in mind. It aims to provide guidance and instruction found and documented in the word of God about our journeys and positions of our mindset that we take and find ourselves as we go. I want all of the readers' of this book to be encouraged that there is and will be glory after this, and you will find you through the word of God.

Introduction

Hello, if you're like me, you are wondering, "Why am I here?" have I even begun to tap into the potential that I possess. Sometimes, you feel like a rat in a maze never really reaching the cheese that seemingly is just around the corner; however, the more and more you search you just really can't seem to find it. Maybe you're looking in the wrong place, the wrong book, searching and playing the wrong game----lol, watching the alignment of the wrong stars. Maybe you're placing the focus on something that just isn't a reality. Maybe discovering you lies in a power that is greater than you. Maybe you can't find or even reach the potential or the true purpose of your life because you really don't know your life or who it is that you have been created to be or even glorify. Maybe you're just looking in the wrong book, trying to get self-help, get perfect schemes that add up to be nothing., leaving your life in a more shallow and unfulfilling cone that is void of the reality that was created for you to live.

If you have found yourself like this, then you're reading the correct book. Yes, you stumbled across something that is going to make and assist you in finding the potential that has innately been given to all of us. It was just a matter of taping in.

Like you, I spent most of my childhood and adult life searching for reality, searching for ways to capitalize on the potential I had always known had been given to me. Finally, the search was over, the search of looking for potential, trying to find a picture that fit the formalities that I was going through. When suddenly, all I had to do was pick up a book, a book that contained sixty-six books full of power-packed stories that relayed to me what the potential that I was looking for was all about. My journey to finding my potential all came to an end when I found me. You, like everyone else in the world, are in a constant quest to find answers relating to who you are and who you were created to be. Like a crazed animal in a room that has no windows and no doors, you scramble to find something to see, some little break that would give you a peek into what is going on in your life. We all have experienced that little instance where we can't find what we want, we can't see any purpose, we can't even discover any reason for going through the things we face. If you're like me you just sit b? What edifying will result from this? How is this to mesh with the story that is being written about my life?

We face hard times, times in which we just run from here to there trying to find answers, trying to find peace that would let us know that there's a plan in all of this. There is no reason to throw in the subliminal towel of life and call it quits. There is a reason to keep on running even though the rain beads are blinding our eyes, and sight is getting further and further away from us. There is a light at the end of the tunnel, but why does the tunnel have to last so long? Why does the tunnel seem like its getting narrower and narrower as I go through it? Why does it seem like reality and fate are against me? Well, that seems to be all of our destined but undesired fate. However, when we open the Word of God, no matter where we are in the globe you can find solace in knowing that He has you just where He wants you.

Chapter 1
Unleashing the God-Given Potential

Job 23:10 lets us know that He knows the way that we must take, and after we have been tried by the fire, it is only then that we will come out as pure gold. We have to be tested and tried, and it's going to cost us something for some maybe sleepless nights, for some maybe being lonely, but nonetheless it will cost. Joshua 3:4 talks about the children of Israel crossing the Jordan. It says, " Early in the morning, Joshua and all the Israelites set out for Shittim and went to the Jordan, where they camped before crossing over…..Joshua said to the priests, "take up the ark of the covenant and pass on ahead of the people" Tell the priest who carry the ark….in essence when you follow all of the instructions given by the Levitical priests you will know what directions to go since you have never been this way before. Quoting that scripture to let you know that there will be instructions that you will need to follow but the promise is after this, there will be glory. You will know what direction to go in to "Find you."

God created us all to have dominion over the things that creapeth on the earth, everything, even the fowls of the air. It is up to us to realize the power that we have living on the inside of us. Ephesians 3:10 states that our God is able to do exceedingly and abundantly above all that we can ask or think according to the power that worketh in you. In this, Paul lets us know that the power is in you, the power to speak to the mountain, and it shall move. Some theologians would argue if it was a physical mountain or just a spiritual mountain, I tend to say that I don't care what kind of mountain it is as long as I can speak and it be moved; that is good enough for me. The power and the potential is ours, we must maximize, capitalizing on its benefits. Nothing in this life will be given to us, God lays out a blueprint a roadmap if you will to follow. Acts 1:8 says "and after that the Holy Ghost has come upon you, you shall be witnesses unto me, in Judaea, Samaria and to utmost parts of the earth. The potential that we have locked on the inside of us is that strength that will propel us to the ends of the earth. We can't unlock the potential to reach the ends of the earth if we haven't unlocked the potential to get us to Samaria.

God has given, just like in the opening lines of the constitution, rights and freedoms that we need and must use if we are to live successful lives in this present world. Our marriages, finances, and everything that we possess are tied to it. It becomes of the utmost importance that we realize this and stop living beneath the God-given potential. God knows the power that is in us; he knows what and how much He can trust us with. Certain things God has made accessible to us through His Son, and certain things we will have to access through our belief and faith in Him. God knew Peter; after all he was the one whom He called "Rock," the meaning of the name Peter. In paraphrasing, God begins to say the devil has set up a trap for you Peter; he is desiring to sift you as wheat. However, I have interceded for you that your strength fails not. I want you to realize the potential that is within you and after you have realized the job that you have to encourage your brother. Just like Christians today, circumstances in life want to trip you, so you do not discover your God-given potential. However, God is saying that we must wake up and realize that He has given all things that pertain to life and happiness and encourage our brother. We can't begin to wallow in self-pity because of things that the enemy has blindsided us with. God has invested too much in us for that. We must keep it moving!

In our quest to find and unlock our God-given potential, we must know what favor is and when it has properly been bestowed upon you. Favor is not something that someone does for you that you couldn't have done for yourself. It is when someone on earth does something for you, and you could have perfectly done it for yourself. Favor is not something that you get because you have done everything the correct way. Favor is not something that you receive because you are worthy; it is not something that you get because of your name or because of the lineage that you have. It is not something that you receive because you have paid for it; a favor is not something that can be bought. It does not have an ending period; as a matter of fact, it's hard to tell when it begins. You just know that it is there and that you are experiencing it. Webster defines favor as "to do kindness for, to use gently, to spare to be pleasing to one's advantage. To regard with favor, approve or like. It means to support, it means to look upon with regard, to show kindness. So, we must understand what favor is to unlock the God given potential. God has favored those that are His, those that will do His will, and those who will honor and bestow Him with His glory.

We must be willing to be obedient to Him in our quest to unlock the potential that He has instilled in us. He says in scripture that He has given us all things that pertain to life, He tells us in Isaiah 54:17 that "No weapon that is formed against shall be able to prosper and every tongue that rises against us in judgment shall be utterly condemned for this is the heritage of the servants of the Lord and the vindication is of me." Most Christians today feel that God doesn't have a plan for us. He knows the potential that we have. This is why He is able to say that the deliverance is of Him. We must be willing to do and tap into the God-given potential that we have. Letting it lie dormant in our bodies is a misinterpretation of God's mercies toward us. Joshua 1:8 tells us that we must observe to do everything that is commanded in God's word, for in doing so, we will make our way prosperous and lead us to good success. We have our entire future in our hands. God tells us that we will make ways to be prosperous and lead us to good success, he knows this, and if we follow this scripture in Joshua, then what He instructs Jeremiah to tell us in 29:11 is reality. "For I know the thoughts and the plans that I think toward you, for they are for good and not for evil to bring you a future and a hope." Jer. 29:18.

We can begin to bless the Lord at all times because we know that God has instilled in us what we need to live successful lives for Him. If we don't live a successful life, it is not because He didn't provide the tools. Deuteronomy 28:9 Says, "The Lord will establish you as a holy people to Himself, just as He has sworn to you if you keep the commandments of the Lord your God and walk in His ways. 10. Then all people of the earth shall see that you are called by the name of the Lord, and they shall be afraid of you." So, you see, even your enemies will be afraid of you if you live according to what the Lord ordains. The power is in our hands. It becomes evident that sometimes we don't live the victorious life because we simply don't want to suffer to do it according to His plan. Romans 8:28 states, "and we know that all things work together for the good, to those who love the Lord and are the called according to His plan. "Simply put, it means that all things will work for those that are walking in His statutes and are fitting into His plans is you will. We have all the power that we need.

He instructed Peter that the keys to the kingdom were given to Him, and he had the authority to bind and loose. How do we activate this power, though? How long will this power last?

We can access the things of God by getting into the things of God. For it is by the things of God that we can hold to a better understanding of the mind of God. Don't get us wrong, we will never be able to totally fathom the things that God has prepared for those who believe and love Him. However, through revelation knowledge, some of God's plan can be shown to us as His servants. In Deuteronomy 28:15, He starts out by telling us that we have charge over our destiny. We have this charge through obedience to Him. However, if we suffer to be disobedient to Him, He tells us nothing but heartache will befall us. So, when it comes to unlocking the God-given potential, the choice is ours. I lay before you Good and Evil choose ye this day whom you will serve will it be God or man? The choice is yours.

Chapter 2
You Co-Own Your Destiny

Has anyone ever had dreams? Have you ever aspired to things you wanted to partake in when you grew up? Were there any doors that you always dreamt that would open for you? Do you have any ideas that you would daydream about and just wish that you would meet the right people to help? Well, God has always let us know that He knows the thoughts and the plans that He has for us. However, to access those thoughts that He has which are good. We must always be open to going after it. God has always let us know that we can be successful, but it is not just going to be dumped in our laps. He instructed the children of Israel, "Enlarge the place of thy tent, Strengthen the stakes." Emphasizing the believer's need to act. I want to tell you it will not be dumped into your laps. I am a living testimony to the fact if you want anything in the realm of success, you must go for it. The same goes for spirituality. He states that things only come by fasting and praying; if we want God's best, we must give Him our best. Do what He says in the word, for in doing this, you make your way prosperous, and it leads you to good success.

In I kings 18, Elijah, the man of God, tells his servant to go and look for rain; we find that he looked several times before he found it. Seven times to be exact. We must realize that if the first time we look for success in life, we may not find it. God says get up! Go try again. Every time is not going to be the right time, however, one will. We must not get discouraged when we don't find it the first time. Galatians 6:9 says that we must not be weary in well doing for we shall reap in due season if we faint not. The season for you to realize the potential that God has for you may not be there yet, but it will. Keep going, keep it moving! I understand family members, naysayers, may design life for you; they may tell you things like give up, you won't make it, and if it hasn't happened yet, it won't. Just like a garden, you have to water it more than one time for it to grow. The destiny that is prepared for you is far greater than just one chance or one shot at whether it will happen or not. So many writers hadn't gotten to the point of being best-selling writers by being discouraged and stopping. Don't quit it will work this time!

I am reminded of a passage of scripture also found in the book of Kings; it gives us a setting that many would say was hopeless; however, it is in this setting that we find out God's will. It states that a widow woman had debts that were owed and, in an effort to have that situation resolved, she consulted the man of God for a resolution. It goes on to tell us that the man of God asked, "What did she have in her house?" she stated a little oil. He instructed what she needed to do with that oil. In hurrying the story, she did as she was commanded and she had enough to pay the debt and live off. I stated that to say this, don't hang up the gift that God has given and take it for granted, as she did the oil. It may be the very thing that brings your deliverance. You may ask what does this have to do with going back and not giving up. The point is when you take things for granted, you stop trying, you stop seeing if it will work. God says, don't give up now; try again. It will work this time! The bible records that the man went several times to see if rain was going to fall, it states that he went a total of six times even though he didn't see anything, it failed to go. We may not see everything fall in line with what God has decreed. However, just because we don't see it doesn't mean that God didn't say it. The bible recorded the seventh time he came back and said I see a little cloud in the shape of a man's hand. Even though he smelled the rain, he didn't see it. You can get ever so close to your blessing you know it's coming, you can taste it, so to speak, but you don't see it. Don't give up! Remember, you are the co-owner of your destiny.

Don't be entrapped by what the enemy says won't happen. If you are an heir to the covenant of promise, it's for you. God has set you aside, the world is not your system, financial system or medical system. You must realize you are a foreign descents. Our kingdom is not of this world. The scripture instructs us that we have treasures stored in an earthen vessel; things of this world are not for us. We serve a higher power, that's why the scripture Romans 8:28 says All things, empathically, all things work together for the good of those that love the Lord and are called according to His purpose. Try again. Though the vision tarry, wait for it for it will come to pass and it will not tarry. My God-given potential to be healed is in me, God-given potential to be delivered is in me, and God-given potential to be successful is in me. We have the authority to speak over ourselves encouraging ourselves constantly. You are the co-owner of you destiny.

I remember a passage of scripture in II Samuel that says David encouraged himself in the Lord his God. Paraphrasing David had all of this opposition, people threatening to kill him; I imagine people were doubting his success; everything was against him. The bible states that He encouraged himself. He deemed that he would be successful regardless of what the opposition said to him. He tried again. He didn't hang what was stated to him in the closet and gave up. He tried again. We must realize that we can't give up on our dreams of success, God is saying, "Go again, it will work this time." We must realize that David had every reason to give up on live. He had sinned against God and nature by having someone else's husband killed, committing adultery, and losing a baby after all this suffering. He tried again. The sword never left his house as a result of him and what he did. He tried again.

We must not give up on our possibilities, what God has for us. The worst things in life makes the best results when we let God take charge. We are co-owners of destiny. Try again, it will work this time! David was almost killed several times by a king who didn't want him to take possession of what was rightfully his; all of this was because of the things that he did. He suffered some of his children to be killed, raped by his own family members. Seeing this discouraging information he still did not give up. I am telling you not to give up it will work this time!

Our potential lies in our own bellies. The book of James tells us that the power of death and life lies in the tongue. This is why I say that we co-own our destiny. The path in life that we take depends on what we speak, belief and follow. God says that He will lead us into all truths, however we must move and make haste on following the things of God. Success will not just fall on us because we serve Him. Success is not going to feel sorrowful that we haven't had a turn to experience it. God tells us to occupy until He comes, simply put do business. The scripture instructs that we are to be men in business. We must explore those opportunities that God has given for it to work. If it doesn't happen the first time; try again it will work this time! Unlocking the potential requires work, it requires activity on our part and consistency is a must. Personal testimony I started school in the fall of '94 as a political science major; I did some things that got out of the plan that God had for me and as a result, had to drop out.

A span of almost 11 years went by, and I still had no degree, this was something I wanted badly. I knew that I wanted it and the degree was something I had to have. I returned to school in 2007 and stayed there. I was told I couldn't do it, and the devil tried to fool my mind; I had opposition death in the family, separation from a spouse I kept going. In May 2013, I became a graduate of Jackson State University and I am currently enrolled in Graduate School at Belhaven University. I didn't give up. I kept trying I knew that it was going to happen, and it did. Don't give up; it will work this time!

Don't get caught in what and who doesn't like you, destiny is not that person. The destiny is yours and you have the responsibility to help make it happen. When our mind becomes right for upward mobility, then destiny becomes a thing that is right around the corner. I remember a passage where a young lady was not received too well, she was not loved and at first began to let that stagnate her. She began to let the fact that she was unattractive become a crutch that caused her to settle for less than God's best. We must not sweat the minors, but we must move on to the things that God has prepared for us. She was doing everything that she thought would make this person love her. This was not going to happen. It wasn't designed for it to be so. We must realize when something is not in the plan for us, we must realize when it becomes time to move on. She did everything she could, but she had to realize that it was time to do what mattered. When she made up her mind that she was going to do what mattered, she became an important part of biblical history. So, what I am saying don't let someone who doesn't count you as important stop you from realizing God's best. Don't allow the enemy to sidetrack you by displaying the mediocre details of life. The factor is what God has for you is far greater than what the devil is displaying. Don't give up. Try again; it will work this time!

Many Christians understand that God has a destiny prepared for them, however they often fail to realize the entire plan. God would that we not lie around doing nothing waiting for destiny to befall us, it won't. Destiny comes to those who are prepared for it. We are the co-owners of our destiny, and it is up to us to follow the plan of God knowing that it is our faith in Him that holds the picture together. He says in the book of Job that He knows the way that we take and after that we have been tried by fire, we shall come out as pure gold. His plan will always work for us; we have to follow it, or else it is not faith. We as Christians, must capitalize on every opportunity to find the place that God wants us to be in. We must prepare ourselves. Destiny does not happen to those who are not prepared to operate in it when it comes. I should not ask God to bless me to be a financer for visionaries when I have not prepared myself in one management class. While we wait for destiny, we must always find ourselves doing something. Reading to advanced adults at residential homes, volunteering at shelters, going to schools and mentoring children is something to build towards the ministry that we desire. We are the co-owners of our destiny. By saying the co-owners of destiny, we trust God to lead us; we present our abilities for Him to work through.

Being not weary in well doing, we shall reap if we faint not. Gal 6:9. Is something that the scripture instructs us to do. Indirectly telling us that it is up to us to work; it might not look like anything is happening but continue. It may not seem that anything is happening but continue to work. The results will come. I seem to remember the scripture instructing in Psalms that we would bring forth fruit in our own season, we must remember the due season will come. The time when all things are paid all debts are settled will come; however, we must work towards the goal. God is there, He has laid out a plan for us to follow. Follow it. Paul instructs and tells Timothy not to neglect the gift that was given him, in other words, he warns him not to give up. The believer must know that they possess the potential that God wants to work with. The scripture in Eph 3:10 says at the end, according to the power that works in us. If we can think it, if we can desire it; thing God is able to bring it to pass. We possess the fuel that it takes to move the car, God however, is the motor that propels it.

We must know that in this walk with Christ. Every opportunity to advance in the kingdom must be capitalized on. Afterall, this is what the kingdom is about advancement. Christ died that He might draw all men to Him, when we neglect the potential that God has placed in us; we fail to fulfill God's plan. Consequently, we become non- advocates of the policies of God. We don't know it but we innately block the fulfillment of scripture. This is heracy. If anyone preaches or teaches any other doctrine, let that man have the spirit of the anti-Christ. God has given the ministry over to us, that is why He saved us; that is why He gave us the keys to the kingdom. If we don't realize our position and potential we become a sounding brass and clanging symbol.

I remember a story of a man named Mephibosheth, this man was lame in his feet. This happened at the hand of someone else. This is the story of how it happened. There was news of an invasion, the nanny for the boy picked him up and ran; she dropped him as she ran injuring both of his feet. I stated this to say that sometimes in life other people will try to hinder us from realizing our God-given potential. However, it is up to us to rekindle the fire that ignites our desire to realize our potential. This man had to dwell there in the land called Lodebar. However, while he was there in Lodebar, he continued to work and do what he was supposed to do. Lodebar was defined as a place of the rock, it was a place where nothing would grow, it was a place known for the non-existence of life.

Nevertheless, this young man lived there. While he lived there, he continued doing what was supposed to do, he was an active participant in his destiny. He worked even though his situation wasn't indicative of him working. However, he worked. He prepared himself for the time God would bless. It is recorded that after time, David summoned him from Lodebar. Being summoned from Lodebar, he was placed at the king's table there he ate with the king and was made a landlord. We must be consistent, even though we don't feel like it, we don't like the place that we are in, and we don't like probably what we are doing. However, we must understand that God has a plan. We must understand that He is ordering things to work in our favor.

However, we must do our part. Be a participant in our destiny. You are the co-owner of your destiny. No matter what the enemy or anyone else says, you co-own and sign your destiny. Your creditability with God offers opportunities for your advancement in Him. Are you dedicated to the things that God says? I am saying it's about the doctrines of your religious institution, I talking about the reality of what dedication is. The reality of what dedication is, is the dedication to the things that are written in the holy bible. There are man-made doctrines that we know overseers expect us to follow. However, I am talking about the things that God says. To unlock your God-given potential, you need to be a discerner concerning those things that are Godly and righteous. Be clear and concise about what it is that you need and desire from God.

While you wait on those things from Him, do just what the word means: "WAIT" on Him. Do as you would if you were working as a waiter in a restaurant. Wait on the customer. Consistently, ask yourself what God wants, do you need more drinks, napkins? Are you doing ok? WAIT on Him. It may seem hard and seem like it's never coming to fruition, but WAIT on Him. All the work that you can do to better God's cause do that. The scripture instructs paraphrasing, "What you may happen for others' God will cause to happen for you." Years and Years, you may have to petition God about that thing that you desire but WAIT on Him. Once we learn how to wait on God we perfect patience. This is a key to unlocking the God-given potential. You can begin to look back on your life and say, "I didn't know that I possessed the ability to wait, but now I see I do."

To unlock our God-given potential, we must be prepared to take risks. However, we must understand that consulting God in what we are doing is paramount. What I mean by taking risks is based on the word of God we must be willing to "Launch out into the deep." Hebrews 11:1 says, "Now faith is the substance of things hoped for, the evidence of things not seen." We can't see the success in what it is we are launching for, but based on the word of God we believe him for the thing we hope for. He instructs us in his word paraphrasing, "and nothing shall be impossible to them." We can't see God working them out for us, we can't see God providing ways for us, we can't see God causing all things to work together for our good, but we must base on the word trust Him for those things we hope for. We must know that we hope not in absent hope but hope that is full of certainty by the word of God. Being assured of what we believe, we stagger not at what it is God has spoken to us, and this is what we hope in. God has given us a key to the dreams in Him, and we have the power through faith to unlock it.

One writer of a song stated, "Prayer is the key to the kingdom and faith unlocks the door." That is the same thing in potential. We must pray in order to receive God's divine direction and then we must possess faith to unlock those directives we receive in prayer. Building a prayer life is something that we must do to unlock God-given potential. We get discouraged because of the things that we don't have, but a prayer life doesn't let us die in it. It brings us back to reality, if you will. It becomes the livelihood and life support when the enemy feels he has the upper hand.

I stated that Cain had a brother named Abel, who offered God an honorable sacrifice in the discourse of time. Cain, out of jealously, killed Cain. Cain later had a son whose name was Enoch, the bible records that Enoch's father built a city and called that city Enoch, later known as the city of Enoch. Enoch pleased God, which defeated the works of the former, his father. You see the devil may try to make you think you will never reach the God-given potential, but the story is not over if you can just bear to WAIT on the second part of the story. You see when Cain killed Abel, the enemy thought it was over, he got back at God. He didn't realize that God is God and He always has another plan. He made sure no one killed Cain so that He could be the father of Enoch. This became a slap in the devil's face because Enoch pleased God. Not only he but the entire inhabitants of his city. Romans 8:28: "And we know that all things work together for the good to those that love the Lord, and are the called according to His purpose." Whatever the enemy has devised for you not to reach your potential God has the turnaround.

We must know that God always has the anecdote for the problem of depression that the enemy brings related to our potential. Hearing from God becomes paramount in our quest to unlock the potential that God has for our lives. We must always be apt to listen to His direction and His words for us, He talks but do we listen. It is for us to listen, pause and WAIT on Him, and you will unlock it. "Now unto Him that is able to do exceedingly abundantly above all that we can ask or think according to the power that worketh in us." Eph 3:10. If we don't believe it, we can't excel in it. If we don't unlock it with our faith to activate it, the formula that God has given to obtain it will not work. Opening a checking account, you always receive a debit card, that debit card however, will not work unless you call an activate it. The same as with the promises of God, we must believe God concerning his promises to activate what is in Duet. 28:9

What good is potential without activating the ability to possess that potential? You guessed it nothing. The world and the things that God has placed in the world for saints to enjoy; but your belief to obtain those gifts depends on you. It depends on YOU!!!!!!

"Now unto Him who is able to keep you from falling and present you faultless before the presence of His glory with exceeding joy to the only wise God our father be glory and majesty, honor and power both now and forever." God has the power to keep us from falling, however it is up to us to access that power. God will not and never has forced anything on us; if we fail Him He is faithful and just to pick us back up; know that He is able to keep us from falling. We must access those things if we don't, we become our worst enemy in achieving our God-given destiny.

Knowing your worth, knowing your worth, is pivotal in reaching your God-given potential. Once you know who you are and what wealth you possess, you put yourself in a better position to achieve your God-given potential. God has given worth to everyone, paraphrasing scripture, "God has given everyone a measure of faith." the measure of faith instills worth in us, it instills integrity in us. God gives us names when we explore the arena of Christendom, we must realize that once God calls us out of a sinful life, he gives us a different name. We can find an explanation for this in scripture, Simon was a disciple but Simon was his surname, meaning the name given by his parents. Jesus gave him another name and changed his name to Peter meaning "rock" in saying this we all have a God-given name. We must realize the worth that is in that name, when we realize the worth that is in our God-given name, we can excel towards the potential that God has given us. The reason why excelling towards God-given potential is so much easier to do is because when we research and find our God-given name it interprets where God desires for us to go. When he however, interprets where it is that He wants us to go we will get there. We must be dedicated to doing some research and lots of prayer to discover this. It just doesn't come. After all, God would not invest that much in us if our potential was going to be that easy to reach. When we know the worth that we possess, we won't be open to doing everything that is offered to us, we won't be so privileged to accept every word that is given to us. We want to prove our integrity to God. We are not trying to see ourselves as the reason for everything, but we understand that the potential that is instilled in us belongs not to us it belongs to God.

The contrary to what most think, it is until we lose ourselves that we discover the highest potential that God has instilled in us. When I can say I don't want to have money, I can say I have it, but so I can establish the ministry of compassion here on earth. When we can say I don't want to preach to establish my ministry but a ministry for the kingdom. When we can say if I don't ever speak or preach again, it doesn't matter I just want the kingdom to prosper, then we have found our God-given potential. You see, the God-given potential is giving God the glory, understanding what we were created to do. That is to worship God. Worship our creator. Once we find ourselves in a position where nothing else matters but the pleasure of the father, we have discovered our God-given potential. Once I can deny myself accurately and allow God not myself to be elevated. I have discovered my God-given potential. God has to be the source of the highest point in which you want to be, nothing else should matter. When nothing else matters, my feelings, my emotions nothing then than when we are elevated towards the God-given potential.

Sacrificing myself in obedience to Christ, the excellency of the cross is more important than anything else. I remember when there was a well that King David longed to have a drink of water out of, he told his mighty men and his mighty men in obeisance to the king went to get the water; upon making it back King David poured that water out. He stated that "If the men thought that much of him to risk their lives and get it, who would he be to drink it." In other words, David did not want to put that much esteem on his own life as to risk someone else's. We have to be sold out to God like that. We have to value His initiative over our own. We have to love a life for Him more than a life of our own. We must lose our lives in order to gain our lives. Once we are willing to do this the God-given potential can be realized. It is once we humble ourselves that we will be exalted.

Know what God has placed in you, know what the word says about you. Joshua 1:8 says, "This book of the law shall not depart out of thy mouth, but thou shalt meditate therein day and night, that thou mayest observe to do according to all that is written therein; for then thou shalt make thy way prosperous, and then thou shalt have good success."

The bible tells us that if we seek Him in this we can co-sign our destiny. Deuteronomy 28 states, "and it shall come to pass, if thou shalt hearken diligently unto the voice of the Lord thy God, to observe and to do all his commandments which I command thee this day, that the Lord thy God will set thee on high above all nations of the earth; and all these blessings shall come on thee, and overtake thee if thou shalt hearken unto the voice of the Lord thy God." Know what He says about you, it makes the journey better.

Chapter 3
Value Your worth

In life, we possess many things of value and we will possess many things of value, those things become worthless to us if we don't know how to value them. A man once had coins they were coins from many years ago. He even had the first nickel. The nickel was imprinted with the buffalo on it, he had several red printed two-dollar bills. He vowed that he would never depart with the coins however, he never went to anyone to invest time into seeing if they were worth anything. That is about the same with the life that God has graced us with, so many of us rely on others to affirm our worth, we rely on words others' say to validate us, even solidify the things that we do and even visions that we partake in. God doesn't want that he wants us to believe His word so that in doing so we can achieve our own God-given potential. You will never discover and ultimately unlock your God-given potential if you stay in a shy timid state, never really wanting to step to the forefront and realize what is that God has called you to do. The deficiency to accept responsibility is key to a lot of people. I remember in that same story of those valuable coins the man didn't believe that they had value in them, which was one of the reasons he didn't take them to see the value in the coins. We are all given certain unalienable things, God-given talents and gifts that we are responsible to capitalize on and multiply. At the beginning of this book I stated, "We hold these truths to be self- evident that all men are created equal and given certain inalienable rights." Consequently, the potential that we have inside of us will never be realized if we remain in a dormant state relying on others to cite it for us. God wants us to realize it for ourselves. He calls us His children and His children are not challenged people, they can speak for themselves, they can discern for themselves. Afterall, this is why we all have bibles and separate prayer lives. Our potential is the highest point of the ability that God has given to us; it is what He has gifted us with paraphrasing scripture "He gave gifts to men." We must tap into that avenue and discover those gifts that God gave to men. We must unlock the hidden potential that God has given us; it is not a mystery, it is not a secret, it is not something that God doesn't want us to discover. He wants us to find it. The worth the God has placed in us shouldn't be played with it must be valued, God has greatness in each of us, He has courage in us, He has a lot invested in each of us. Value what it is that God has placed inside of you, it's worth more than you think! Sampson did not value his worth, he was a Nazarite, there was a Nazarite vow that he was born into. He didn't value the Nazarite vow and what it was how important it was to him. You see in the Nazarite vow he could not do several things, he could not touch a dead body, he could not cut his hair among other things. This Nazarite vow was very important for him he was born into a family of spiritual wealth, a family where his mother was barren and she prayed and prayed for a child and God granted her a son. Most often, we don't look at the things that God has gifted us with and we don't have enough gratitude to show any form of appreciation for it. The potential to be holy before God was inside of him, but because of a Philistine, he gave up the value of the worth that was in him. As the story continues, Sampson was introduced to the Philistine woman, he was attracted by her beauty. He was so caught up in showing the brutal strength that God had gifted him with he began to impede into the Nazarite vow. To flaunt the gift that God gave him, he took the jaw bone of an ass to slay foxes. This was a violation of the Nazarite vow, because the ass was dead. Another violation was one day when He was walking along with this Philistine, he touched a dead body, this clearly was in violation of God's law for Nazarites. You see in an effort to show off for someone he adored, he gave up access to the potential that was given inside of him by God. We must be keen to know when the devil is trying to squander us out of the God-given gift that God has created within us. As the story goes on, he begins to play with riddles with the philistine woman when she asks him where his strength lie. You see, we can't realize our potential in Him (God) if we don't obey him, by playing with the devil. We can't play with the devil, human flesh against a prince of the power of the air, the devil will always win. We can't hold fire in our bosom and not get burned, this is what the bible instructs us. The story goes on that when taunted over and over by the enemy, Sampson gave up his secret. Once he gave up his secret, things began to be overturned. The devil had that victory in the life of Sampson. Sampson's potential was given up and it was given up by Sampson himself. He didn't value the worth of his Nazarite vow. The Philistine army came in, they bound Sampson's arms but like always Sampson tried to break away. However, the power to break loose was not there anymore, his eyes were gauged out. The story ends with

Sampson working in the Philistinian court grinding meal. It occurred in the dispensation of time that the Philistines had a party were Sampson worked. Sampson began to pray to God, he prayed that God would grant him strength one last time. Sampson made his way over to two pillars lodging himself in between them, there he began to push. He pushed and the pillars broke, causing a lot of Philistines to die. Even because Sampson didn't value his worth enough to wait until he could discover his God-given potential he slayed more Philistinians than he did in his entire career. Sampson's potential was realized by default. We can't realize our God-given potential by default meaning after we have gone contrary to the will of God then we come around afterward. However, we must seek to be of continued service to Him before we find ourselves in trouble. Many stumbling blocks in life try to hinder us from realizing the potential that God has in us. We see Peter was a good example. He was called "rock" by the savior but at the end he was entrapped by the enemy. So much to the point that he started to swear that he didn't even know the Messiah. Jesus told him that before the cock crows twice he would deny Him thrice, and it happened just as Jesus said that it would. Peter was able to ultimately realize the potential that God had in him, however, he had several instances where he was tricked by the enemy. There was the centurion soldier, he cut off his ear; there was the woman who made the connection between him and the Messiah, he started to swear that he didn't know him. So, you see, if we would just be willing to suffer with him, we can reign with him. David did some things that caused a sword to be in his household, the scripture says that he saw a man's wife on the balcony and he began to lust after her, she would later become David's wife. David was the king so he put the woman's husband on the front line of the army, this soldier's name was Uriah. The scripture goes on to record that David and Beersheba would conceive a son, this son would not live. Over time the bible says that David did nothing during the entire time, he didn't eat, nothing. When the son died, it is recorded that David got up and began to do things, He stated that God was good to him in that He allowed the sin to leave from him. So you see, the potential that could have been realized earlier would have come into existence earlier had David not had to take a detour. Because of his actions of disobedience, he had to wait on blessings later on, the bible records that there was another son that was conceived, and that son was named by God, "Jedidiah" whom Jehovah loves. This son would be known as Solomon, the greatest and wisest to ever live. The potential was realized but it could have been realized much earlier in his life had he not took his detours. David was crowned King of Israel which was his potential that God had in him, but he couldn't rightfully take his place in the potential, because he was busy reaping some of the rewards from the wrongs that he did. Value your worth. If you know that God has called you to greatness don't do anything that will jeopardize that. There is worth that is in you value it. Don't play Russian roulette with the destiny that God has prepared for you. There was a woman named Rahab, she was able to realize the potential that God had for her, she was able to house the men of God while they were going out to spy on Jericho. The bible records that she houses the men of God while some of the enemies were looking for them, the bible states that she drove a spike through their temples while they were sleeping. She realized the potential that God placed her in the right place at the right time. She realized that it was not a greater time than that of the present, she realized that she probably would have died anyway if it would collapse. She realized that she was going to do what was right, she was going to spare the men of God. The bible says that she later joined the Israeli people and became one with them. She began to worship their God. She realized the potential that was inside of her, by surrendering herself to the plan of God. We have to realize when it's God's time to be manifested in our lives, he has a plan for us if we could just be still and listen. If we would just use reasoning. God is there with us all of the time waiting for us to walk into His plan that is going to provide a destiny for us. We sometimes spend our entire lives looking for ways to fulfill the potential it is that God has for us, but if we just stop and listen to his direction we will get the plan. Value your worth, the bible tells a story about a man named Ahab. this man named Ahab was married to a very cunning and evil woman named Jezebel; this woman was able to charm anything and anyone under the spell of her satanic charm. We know as the story goes her husband Ahab wanted to possess land that did not belong to him, this land belonged to a man named Naboth. When we confronted Naboth about the land, Naboth refused to give or even sell the land you see the land belonged to his family. It is recorded that Naboth went home, and across the bed he laid and wept. When Jezebel asked what was going on, he told her that Naboth would not sell him the land, Jezebel in all of her evil and craftiness, said leave him to me. She would later have Naboth killed just to take the land, she took the land and delivered it to Ahab. She would later suffer because of that; the bible states that hunger ate her at the wall of Jezreel. However, Ahab recognized that God was the sovereign God and that He controlled everything. Ahab began to cry out before the Lord, and the Lord saw how Ahab began to humble himself before the Lord. God spoke to his prophet to tell Ahab that because he humbled himself before the Lord God, he would not let judgment come upon him, but it would go to his generation spans and they would suffer the judgment. Ahab realized that his potential would be realized if he surrendered to God, he recognized that the Lord was God thus realizing the potential that God placed in him. You see sometimes people are forced into being evil by those we are surrounded by, God sees the potential that we have in us, it is up to us to realize the fullest potential in us. God knows that it's there. We must be smart and wise enough to realize it. The evil and controlling spirit of Jezebel was designed to control everything that she encountered, however Naboth did not know what her plans were; he did not suffer the penalty for her sins because he acknowledged God as being Lord. When we fully value and acknowledge our worth we must be prepared because the enemy is going to set up boundaries for us; however, it is up to us not to let those boundaries be the thing that hold us captive.

I am reminded of a story in II Samuel, and it is very pertinent to knowing your worth and your value. There was a young child named Mephibosheth who was wounded at a young age, he was lame in not one but both of his feet. The first thing that we must learn is that the devil wants to stop us from walking to our destiny, he figures that if he can wound you in both of your feet, then you won't be able to walk towards your destiny. The story goes on to tell us that he was dropped and wounded by his nanny at the tender age of five years old, it is quintessential that we understand that the devil wants to lay hold or claim on our lives while we are young and feeble, for when we get older we will have developed a prayer life and can ward him off. So the devil tries to get us when we are young and ruin any hopes that we have for a future in Christ. "For I know the thoughts and the plans that I have for you for they are for good and not for evil to give you a future and a hope" Jer. 29:11.

THE DEVIL DESIRES TO HANDICAP YOU

The devil may have tried to hinder you, he may have tried to wound your feet to stop you from walking toward your destiny. However, No weapon will ever be formed against you that will prosper, God says that every tongue that exalts itself in judgment against you shall be utterly condemned. God wants you to know that even though the devil may have tried to wound you and stop you from walking to your destiny, God's grace is sufficient and it found you. Glory be to God!! His grace was looking for you when the devil wounded you and forced you to live in a homemade town called "Lodebar", God's grace found you. When the devil said no, God in fact said yes. He wounded you, tried to take your joy away, tried to take your peace away, this joy that you have the world didn't give it you and furthermore, My God shall supply you with the peace that surpasses understanding and it will guide your heart and mind in Christ Jesus.

DON'T ALLOW THE DEVIL TO HI-JACK YOUR DREAMS

Yes, the devil tried to wound you, but God healed you, and by His grace he says get up!!! Unlock the potential in you. Unlock the dream again, unlock the vision again, unlock the day dreams again, unlock the gift that God has given you. Rush into life again, and don't let your dreams become stale with the air of life, the shelf life on your dreams has not run its course, your dreams have not expired, your dreams can be resurrected, it can live again, it can breathe again, it can come to fruition. Don't let the devil gainsay you; don't let the devil tell you that it is finished. Jesus is the only that can say it is finished and he did that over two thousand years ago. So blossom again, let your flowers bloom again, let your heart love again, let your feet move to the beat of God's drum again. Unlock it, Unlock it, Unlock it.

DON'T LET LIFE PLACE IN A MENTAL STATE OF LODEBAR

Life found Mephibosheth in Lodebar, Life found Mephibosheth in misery, Life found Mephibosheth in the presipice of a bad time. That is where the devil desires to put you. Mephibosheth found himself dealing with life and life and coping with the fact that he was a king's grandson and was now forced to live out the rest of his days in this cold, wretched, and disturbing place, the place where nothing grows the place where life doesn't exist, the place where nothing is edible, the place where photosynthesis and osmosis don't take place the place where life is not good, life is not well, life is in agony when the night falls and you hate the next day that you are destined to enter. However, the king found him, and the king brought him up from Lodebar to his table. This is what God wants to do for you, he wants to bring you out of Lodebar, no more time for Lodebar, no more time for the same ole stuff, no more time for the run around that is in Lodebar. God wants to unleash you from the Lodebar experience.

We must know our worth, we know our value, we know who we are in Christ, and we know that God has designed us for exactly what it is that we are presently doing. "For I know the way that you must take and after you have been tried by fire that you shall come out like pure gold." God is the only way that you can discover your value, your passion, your desire and who is the desire of your heart. It is only when you realize this that you will unlock your God-given potential.

STAY IN TOUCH WITH GOD'S VISION FOR YOU

I am reminded of a person in a story who was forced to approach Jesus because of others who spoke of stoning her. She had lost the potential to see the value in her life, even though she faced sudden death the reality of who she was had interwoven into who she had become. She lost the reality of who God created her to be, she lost the meaning of true worth and true value. Jesus reminded this daughter of who she was, he reminded this daughter not of what life made her but of who He made her to be. Sometimes in life we find ourselves tangled up in what life has made of us. It is not our experiences that make us, it is our value that God gives us that makes us. However, he had to remind her that there was only one thing that separated her from everyone else in the world and that was sin. However, that sin did not make her, that sin did not validate who she was, and that sin did not determine her future. He just spake to her and said, "Go and Sin no more."

Sometimes, all God has to say to us is "Go and Sin no more." When God says, "Go and Sin no more," we know He has given us a brand-new start. We can realize our true value or true worth. "Go and Sin no more."

When we realize the true potential that God has placed on our lives, then we can live as God wants us to live, the acceptable will of God. "Be not conformed unto this world, but be transformed by the renewing of your mind, that you may prove what is that good, perfect and acceptable will of God." God wants us to present our bodies to Him so that He can use us for His will and His glory, God wants to bless us with His glory so we can tell His wonderful story of how we have overcome the world even-though opposition faced us on every hand but we made it over.

Chapter 4
Know your Worth

In our quest to unlock the true potential that God has for our lives we must be certain of who and whose we are, we must stand firm in the fact that God has called us and He has equipped us for the journey. I remember a story of a man in the bible, this man after having his territory that was given to him by a king named Aschish, he found himself having to encourage himself in the Lord, the story goes on to explain that he went before the Lord asking if should overtake or rather should he go to battle with them, the Lord told him that he should go and it was certain that he would recover all. The scripture states that he put on his royal garments and made the decision to go to war.

RECOGNIZE WHO YOU ARE

It is my take that nothing happens until we recognize who we are, God can tell us all day that we can possess a thing but it is until we make the conscious decision in our mind to get up an overtake that thing it will never come to fruition. God has given us the power to overtake things that we know that we should right-fully have. However, if the enemy can ever take the identity away from us, he can begin to sneak in an take those things that God says that we can have. Sometimes, it is not a sneak, we just openly give our identities over to the devil.

CLAIM YOUR IDENTITY

David had to make the decision to get up and take his territory back, he had to come to grips with who he was, who God had called him to be. God has called all of us to be rulers having dominion over every creeping thing, and no matter what the situation in our lives is, we must know that God has called us to greatness. He has called us to mirror him. When we properly engage ourselves with those garments that indicates who we are then we are ready to overtake it. David was the king and it was until he became aware of who he was that he would able to do what God instructed him. Some of us know that God has called us to a specific assignment, but the garments are being clothed by dust, and they are being clothed by dust because we won't step up to who we know we are and put on those clothes. Back in biblical times, clothing was an implication of a lot of things, it portrayed status and kingship, and if you walked in that vein then you wore the clothing that represented that.

PUT ON YOUR GOD-GIVEN CLOTHES

God wants us to put the redeemed clothing on, that is why He tells us to put on our strength because it is symbolized by clothing. Speak with authority the authority that God has given us in our clothing, purple royalty garments. God tells us that we are a royal priesthood and a chosen generation that we might show the righteousness of the one who has called us from the darkness and brought us into the marvelous light. He wants us to depict what he has called us to be in Him. Delivered, set free, knowing the true potential that He has given us.

DECIDE WHOSE AGENDA TO PURSUE

Another instance in scripture is where a person had to discover the agenda of what it was that they were supposed to do, what they were designed for, and what the purpose of the position that God allowed them to experience. Ester rose to a life that would later challenge her to discover the potential and the God-given treasure that was to make her people successful people. The story begins when queen Vashti was deposed for not coming when the King summoned her which began the quest to find another queen. Suppose we would discover that God has a plan for everything that he allows in our lives. In that case, we will find less and less that we have to experience because our purpose will become obvious to us. God wants us to find, know and ultimately connect with our purpose. In keeping with the story, the cabinet was instructed to go out and recruit women of beautiful stature and countenance so that they may come and show themselves to the king after they have adorned themselves in presentable manners. You see, for us to know who we are and find our purpose and what God has designed us to be, we have to adorn ourselves in proper attire before we present ourselves to the king, this all comes with knowing who and who we are first. So she went to adorn herself, and she was selected as one that was chosen by the king; she was the next in line to become the queen of the Persian people.

DREAM KILLERS

The scripture lets us know that there were people who lived in jealousy against her, we need to see that when we discover the keys that will ultimately unlock our God-given potential and destiny, there will be haters there will be those out there that desire to sift you, desiring to take the very foundation away from you or out of your hands. There was Hamon, an evil ruler who sought the position of power, but never got it; it is also important to note that there are those who will try to obtain power by means of hatred and jealousy; however God says that promotion comes from the east nor the west He sits one up and takes the other down. So, in keeping with the story, Ester has an uncle whose name was Mordecai, Mordecai became the counselor for Ester to coach her on the ways of conduct. To make this long story short, Ester had to realize what she was there for, she had to realize why she was placed in a high position, she had to realize what the potential was inside of her that until this time was lying dormant. There was a war waged against the Israelite people, which just happened to be the descent of Ester and her uncle Mordecai; Ester wrestled with the decision of standing in the gap for her people, she was ordained for the time however, it would take someone else to bring out the reality that God had placed on Ester's life. Often times, we need someone who is so in tune with God that they can bring out the message that God is saying to us regarding the purpose of our lives, a Prophet a seer as in the times of old. Ester found herself being a pivotal part of the plan for God's deliverance towards His people Israel, she just had to tap into the potential that God created her to fulfill, she just had to realize that God was going to go before her and not behind her.

CAPITALIZE YOUR ASSIGNMENT

She unfortunately had to have someone to come to her and talk to her and then she would realize what the assignment was for her to do. Mordecai was that person, in our lives, we need someone who can bring the plan of God to us, to pry our minds. We can get so caught up with the daily trials and going of this life that we fail to acknowledge what God has us here for. The scripture says, "And we know that all things work together for good to those that love the Lord and are the called according to His purposes." Rms 8:28, that simply means those that are fitting into His purpose and His plan.

NAVIGATION IS KEY

The plan of God is like a jig-saw puzzle or like a maze is to the mouse; we must navigate our way through it; we might get lost along the way we might not find out the necessity of this life, however we can rest assured that there is a plan if we can just make it to tomorrow. The vision that God has for us is one of peace, and He wants us to envision the prosperity that He has for us. The purpose that He has for our lives must be realized that there is potential, and it is a God-given potential and we can unlock it.

GOD HAS GOOD PLANS FOR YOU

Jeremiah 29:11 says, "For I know the plans and the thoughts that I think toward you for they are for good and not for evil, to give you a future and a hope." We should know that the plans that God has for us are good, we just need to only open the God-given potential that He has given to us. Just as at the opening of this book, it was stated that the preamble to the constitution stated that God has given us unalienable rights, rights to life, liberty and the pursuit of happiness.

OVERCOME THE WOUNDS OF LIFE

As stated earlier, Mephibosheth was the son of Jonathan, King Saul's son. The scripture in II Samuel 4 records what happened to Mephibosheth for life to find him in the situation that occurred to him. He was wounded by the person who was directed to take care of him, which brings me to points that I want to make to show you what the devil desires to do to you for you not to value your worth. He desires to diminish the integrity of those you trusted in; he desires to hurt you while you're young, and he desires to cripple you disabling your ability to walk towards your destiny.

GOD HAS THE INFLUENCE IN YOUR LIFE

The scripture states that the nurse who was given charge over Mephibosheth heard tidings that King David was coming, and she picked up Mephibosheth and ran with him, however in her haste to get away the scripture records her dropping him. The bible states that as a result, he became lame in his feet, another translation allows us to know that he became lame in both of his feet. While Mephibosheth was still young the devil compromised the integrity of the person that he trusted in; the devil will use pastors, women of God, men of God, parents who ever he can, mentor people of influence to hurt us, to wound us to make us stop doing what is right, to make us stop doing the things that God has instructed us to do, they make us put God into default in our lives.

ALLOW GRACE TO FIND YOU

God is able to present us in a light that the world knows that grace has found us, just like King David wanted to show the kindness of God to Mephibosheth who was left in the house of Saul; Jesus wants to show us the grace of God. When we realize that Lodebar is a mental place that the enemy desires to put us in but God's grace can find us and deliver us knowing your worth becomes natural.

Know your worth and cease letting the devil make a spectacle out of you; the scripture indicates that you were fearfully and wonderfully made. Don't allow society to make choices for you, choices that you never wanted for yourself; allow God to show you the worth that He has invested in you.

DON'T LET SOCIETY MAKE YOUR DECISIONS

Scripture indicates in the book of kings that there was a woman and her son who were going to bake the last cake in the household and they were going to die, she had already prepared what she was going to do. Society has already prepared how it is going to make a choice for you, society has already counted you out, but instead of accepting the status quo, let God show you your worth. The widow already made the choice for her son, she already told the man of God that she and her son was going to eat the cake and die, her son probably was persuaded that he was going to believe God for abundance, her son was probably already purposed in his intents that he was going to believe God, and that a change was going to come into the situation. Society wants you to think that its choices are the best for you.

Know your worth, know what God has spoken over you, know that you are the head and not the tail, know that you are above and not beneath, know that you are the lender and not the borrower, know that you are blessed in the city and in the field, blessed when you go in and when you come out. When you know your worth, you won't let the gainsayer entrap you, you won't allow society to demoralize you and tell you what you are not educated, what you are not pretty enough, what you are not skinny enough to do.

DON'T COMPROMISE YOUR WORTH

Know your worth, don't allow someone who has been kicked out of heaven; don't allow someone who doesn't have a second chance at life to tell you that you have no worth. When he tells you that you will never be nothing let him know that you are the righteousness of God, when he tells you that you can do nothing; I can do all things through Christ. When he says that you will never have peace, say my God shall keep thee in perfect when my mind stays on Him. The devil would like to offer you several lies that say that you won't but God tells us one truth, and that's going to hold strong…. YOU CAN!!!!!!

Chapter 5
Re-Building your Worth

Now that you realize your worth re-build your worth. Surround yourself with those people who will pour into you and not constantly and consistently take away from you. You can only pour so much into a jar before it over flows; when God starts to re-arrange the order of friends, don't resist, let him re-build your worth, let Him orchestrate your destiny. Re-build your worth; re-building is good. Re-building will bring new strength to an otherwise old-fashioned space. Re-building will bring a new tower while keeping the character of the original. In re-building, we must clear a new surface; don't re-build the tower upon the old foundations, the scripture instructs us that we can't pour new wine into old wineskins. The reality of that old wine skin was, the fact that it would get to old and not very flexible and as a result, when it would not able to hold what is being poured into it; the wine skin would burst, and the entire substance would be wasted.

David was a man after God's own heart, however he faced a demon of his own, and despite popular belief that the demon was jealousy, scripture indicates that there was something in the City of David called the Ark of the Covenant, the housing place of the presence of God. When trying to move this place, it occurred that the oxen carrying it caused it to tilt; fearing the house of God falling, Uza reached to catch it, and upon doing so, he was stricken dead. Seeing this, David became confused with God and sent the Ark of the Covenant away from the City of David to Obed Edom's house; upon seeing the Ark in his house and the blessings that began to overwhelm Obed Edom's house, David became jealous and wanted the Ark back. It was only after he saw how the covenant blessed Obed's house that he began to dance before the Lord until his clothes were rent, only after he was assured that it was okay.

PRAISE GOD WHILE RE-BUILDING

When re-building the foundation, we must be able to praise God even when he is not blessing our dwelling, otherwise when trouble comes through what God has blessed us with, we will get depressed again and begin to doubt that God is actually in it. We must learn to let all of the pre-conceived notions get out of the way. God is certain, and He wants us to be.

Obed – Edom didn't have anything to do with the reason that God was blessing the house through the Ark of the Covenant. It was just that the presence of God was in Ark. When re-building the foundation, we have to be sure that God is with us no matter what, just like a marriage, it can't be based on or built on the what-if factor, if you will. God wants us sure that we are on His side.

David needed just to petition God and he would have discovered the reason that Uza was stricken, you see only the Levitical Priests were supposed to have dealing with the Ark, only they were designed to burn incense in the holy places of God; so it was because of that reason that he was stricken. We must be knowledgeable of God enough to know that, he doesn't want us to be scared or confused about anything.

God requires us to know what it is that we are getting into, if we can't trust God why re-build? It becomes evident that we must trust him and that is the only way that we can be accurately able to trace him. Just as a marriage is built upon the foundations of trust, we are married to God so to speak and our foundations must be built upon trust in Him and that He knows what is best for us. We must trust God even when we can't trace Him, there are foundations don't have cracks or anything of the sort when we can actually trust him.

RELEASING THE FEAR FACTOR

God requires us to release the fear factors in our lives. God is not a God that instills fear in us, but He is a God of love, and He wants us to know that He is. Scripture indicates that "perfect love casts away all fear." when we can see that God's loves us and He wants the best for us, then we will have no problem releasing the fear factor in our lives.

The devil desires to unleash the fear factor in your life, I recently experienced a situation where the fear factor in my life was unleashed, what I feared the most came upon my family. Through this God let me know that He was a protector, an innovator, and a rejuvenator. He rejuvenated the positive in the situation; yes, the devil was on the job of trying to destroy any inkling of hope, glory to God that perfect love casts out all fear. The fear factor was no longer a factor in my life.

I am not going to say that going through was comfortable, but the coming out made the going through all the more worth it. You have to make the affirmation in your life, "I will not be a victim," I am going to turn the situation around on the enemy. Don't stop what you're doing in God, don't stop looking to him, don't stop treading over un-chartered territory, because the more you do it will distract the enemy and make him, reckon that the sufferings of this present world are not worthy to be compared to the glory that shall be revealed in us" (Rms. 8:18-19, NIV).

Discussed earlier was a story about a young boy named Mephibosheth, who was found by the new king; he thought that the new king was going to kill him but the new king was going to give him the gifts that were rightfully his. As the story goes on when he was finally found, he hid to escape what he thought was sudden death, but when the king got to him, he allowed him to eat his table continually. Mephibosheth was wounded, so he thought that since that bad situation happened to him, anything else would be equally as bad, so in essence he prepared for it. Sad to say we as followers and sinners who are saved by grace sometimes feel the same way, we feel that since society has always given us bad things, and bad things have happened in our lives, that's all that God has to give us. This is not true!

God says that He has come that we might have life, and that we might have that life abundantly, the main purpose of the blood of Jesus was to make us acceptable to God so it is evident that when God sees the blood of Jesus over our lives. He remembers the redemption and tragedy passes over.

Chapter 6
Re-Identifying who you are

King David, in the II Samuel 30 chapter, was heartbroken that the territory given to him by King Achish was destroyed by the Amalekites; not only was the territory invaded but the wives and children were taken captive. It was in this that the bible records that David had to encourage himself in the Lord his God, we must do this also in the face of opposition when the enemy wages all kinds of war against us when the enemy tries to make us take down on what God has told us that He has for us.

The bible records that David encouraged himself, but however, he still didn't know whether he should move or not. The Bible says that he put on his priestly garments and asked the Lord he should overtake the Amalekites. The Lord told him to go, and it was certain that he should and would recover all. You see, it is not until we remind ourselves of who we are and what are assignment is that we can make the decision or if God will speak to us. We must know that God speaks to us concerning what level we are on when it comes to His hierarchy. Sometimes, we wonder why God hasn't spoken to us concerning simple matters, well it's because God speaks to the finished product and not the product that is on the assembly line, so to speak. This is why he could say that David was a mighty man of valor right after he fell into sin. God spoke to the reality of who he was and not at present what he was.

For instance, God may call you rich while you have no car, no house and no money in your pocket, it is because He speaks to what you are in His sight; not what you are in your own sight. God is a God of completion and what He sees when He looks at you is the completion of what He says you shall be. That is why he spoke to the light and called it a day and to the dark and called it a night and it came into being, was because it must be complete as He says it is.

So, we must re-identify who we are in Him, we are no longer in-complete but in reality, we are the completion of what He says we are. As stated earlier when re-identifying ourselves we must recognize who we are what God has called us to be. That what Satan, the accuser of the brethren, Beelzebub or whatever negative connotation we call him wants to do, he wants to rob you of your identity. It's just like our spiritual social security number all of the rights that we have to obtain the things of God, he desires to rob you of that.

When we realize that we have power in Christ Jesus, we have authority under that name we have dominion over every creeping thing under that name, demons begin to flee from us because of the power that we have in conjunction with that name. The bible states that we are heirs of God and joint heirs with Christ, so in essence everything that He has, everything that He is it's mine.

David had to re-identify who he was in Christ, he was anointed to be king. Why would a king have to be scared and fearful about overtaking the people who burned the territory that was given to him? When God gives us territory we have to have the mindset that there is no devil in hell that can take this away from us. We have to know that God has called me to be blessed, blessed in the city and blessed in the field, blessed when you go in and blessed when you go out, blessed to be the head and not the tail, above and never beneath, God tells us. You must never forget that identity, if this occurs, you forfeit what God has for you.

I know the thoughts and the plans that I have for you, says God, plans to prosper, giving you a future and a hope (Jer. 29:11). God has great plans for you but you must know that you are entitled to them, they are yours. Stephen Covey tells us that we must see the end before the beginning (Covey, 2007) and we must believe that God has the best at heart for us.

There was a prophet used of God, he was a mighty man of God, used to restore a woman's son back to life, used to sanctify a pot of poisoned stew, used to call down fire from heaven to burn up the sacrifices to a pagan God. However, when he was faced with opposition, he forgot his identity, he forgot who he was in Christ, and he ran. This is the stale-mate that we don't want to happen, he ran and ran until the angel of the Lord told him to rest, lay under this juniper tree and eat for the journey is too great for you.

He ran, and just like he ran some of us are running, but the potential will never be realized. The potential that we have inside of us if we constantly run from the devil. God has given us the authority to bind things on earth, he instructs us that whatsoever we bind on earth shall be bound in Heaven. Realize the potential!!!

The potential is there, but we have to rebuild our identity to realize it. The devil, throughout our lives has tried to rob us of everything that God has innately designed us to possess. It is just like he has taken our spiritual social security number, everything that is our he has falsely obtained it. Whatever God has told us that we can have the devil has gotten those things from us. We need to gain it back!! Put on your garments, God has given us a garment of praise for the spirit of heaviness. The devil is deceiving us from possessing the best. God wants us to have the best but we must rebuild our identity. Take back what the enemy stole.

The denial of Christ was foretold to Peter, Jesus stated that before the cock crow thrice you will deny me twice. It was apparent that what was going on at that time caused Peter to miss out on the identity he had with Christ. Sometimes we allow circumstances and things that are going on around us to forget the must identity that we have with Christ. Jesus is saying that regardless of what is going on around us it must not cause us to become lost in the identity that we possess.

We must recognize the tricks of the enemy, if we deny the identity that God has given us we fall prey to the enemy. That is what the enemy wants for us, he wants us to deny those things that God has called us to. Peter was in a situation where if he had shown that he was connected to Jesus he would probably have been crucified with Him. So, he denies Him, he denied our Savior, he denied our Lord. In modern day to be relevant to us, Satan wants us to deny that God has called us to greatness, he wants us to deny the fact that God has called us to open doors.

I remember a story where a woman was going through a famine, and when approached by the man of God she stated that she was going to cook a cake for her and her son and they both was going to die. Satan wants to make those decisions for us, he wants us to walk into the confounds of death along with him. The young son may have wanted to try and see what God had for him, he may have wanted to live. However, the decision was made for him. She stated that myself and my son will eat this cake and we are going to die. Satan is saying to people every day, the situation is hopeless so we are going to give up. However, I challenge you to be the one who says I am going to live and not die, I am going to live and see what God has for me, I am going to live and not die.

We have to possess the perseverance that the woman with the issue of blood had, the scripture states that she pressed her way through the crowd and touched the helm of Jesus' garment. Fearing and trembling, she stood in amazement as Jesus turned himself about in the press and stated, "who touched me" (John 11). Seeing how it was so many people in the press the disciples stated with all these people around, how can you distinguish that anyone has touched you. It was a different kind of touch, it was a touch of desperation, it was a touch of anxiety, it was a touch of sweat.

This shows that they are different kinds of touches. In re-building our identity we must present ourselves eager to seek those things for healings from God. She could have faced sudden death, she could have faced public stoning but she took a chance to get her identity back. The Bible says that she had gone all over the world seeking healing but nothing for her betterment was done.

Sometimes we leak our identity out throughout our lives. Sometimes our identities become a part of something that God has never intended for us. Still, she pressed her way through the crowd to get her identity back, she pressed her way through the crowd to get her personality back, she pressed her way through the crowd to get what she lost back.

The devil desires that we never be brave enough to get anything back from the Lord. The enemy desires that we always stay broken. However, the good thing about being broken is that we can always come to God, consequently the devil doesn't want that for us. It is certain for he comes to kill steal, and destroy.

Chapter 7
Re-Strategize, Re-Verbalize, and Re-Mobilize

James wrote in his gospel that we must count it all joy when we enter into divers trials and temptations, he cites that we are going to have trials and tribulations as long as we are in this earthly life; however he tells us to count it all joy. The trials that we are up against we must understand are not designed to take us out, they are not designed to cause us to go into oblivion but they are used as stepping stones to get us to the destiny that God has prepared for us. We must understand that it is not about you but it is about the assignment God has for you.

The assignment that God has called you since birth for to occupy, to minister in He has given you a grace for the assignment that you are supposed to carry out. However, if we allow the situations that we are going through to be about us, then God is not glorified like He wants to be. See the situations that are around you are not for you but for those that are coming after you. The scripture states paraphrasing, that we are surrounded by a great cloud of witness, so people old patriarchs and matriarchs are standing up when you run cheering you on, however, if you give up because you assume the attack is about you, God gets no glory.

The devil uses strategic plans to combat you personally; it's personal but it's not personal because the vendetta is with God, that's who we want to get back at. So, he tries to cancel your assignment so God will not get glory because God kicked him out of heaven a long time ago, yes he's still mad. He wants your assignment. However, you must understand that he can only attack you and try to stop you from the assignment. He is not strong enough to speak into the atmosphere as God can, so he tries to battle against small people like God's children, a spiritual bully. However, tell the devil "My big brother is coming."

The student at the school who desires to be the bully, hits on the students that are small, look like they can't fight, and look like they will always be taken down. However, look at the devil and say "My Big Brother's Coming." I remember when I was in school I wasn't a person to respect fighting, so I didn't try to do it. I wasn't practiced in it, I was more scared than anything. I did a lot of talking. However, I had a big brother, my big brother I knew he was going to get everyone that was messing with me. My big brother would take care of it. I was being pushed by a bully, and I was just saying, "Stop, Stop," but my big brother heard, and when he heard he came running, the bully didn't hear my brother coming and out of the blue, my brother pushed him so hard he hit the ground, crying sorry, sorry!!!!

The devil wants to push you around. The devil wants to push you down. However, when you get the word in you, you have the big brother, Jesus. You can start to speak that word and put the enemy at bay, make the devil say sorry, sorry, sorry! Make the devil wish that he didn't mess with you because you got the big brother, the devil, you can destroy my dream nor my purpose. After all, I got the big brother. Joyful, praise!!!! I got the big brother.

The devil has implemented a strategy to destroy you and thus you have to re-strategize yourself for his attacks. You must develop the most strategic moves that you can to combat the enemy at this time and in this season. The strategy that the Christian must possess is the strategy of prayer. The Bible talks about when the Israelites wanted to seek God concerning anything when they became out of sync, they went to a place called Mizpah, and this is recorded as a place where they sought the Lord. We must strategize and go to our own Mizpeh and begin to seek the face of the Lord again. Re-strategize!!

It was recorded in the annals of history that major shifts in production to grocery stores and major companies began to be successful all because they re-strategized the mode in which they did business. When faced with trials from the enemy, we must re-strategize, find out what our plan will be and then re-strategize and make it happen.

LOVE THE ENEMY OUT OF THE PERSON

Recently, I was in a situation where the enemy was running in a person so bad that everything that they would do was prompted by the work of the enemy. We'd ask God why the person was acting so violently towards us, always escalating the tactics that they would use to aggravate every-day, every-day it was something different. Finally, God spoke and said, "Change your Strategy". You see sometimes you have to love the enemy out of a person.

When you love the enemy out of a person, you are not loving the enemy or the things that he is doing. However, you just see that this is not the person, but it is the work of the enemy operating through the person; so you love the enemy out of the person. Some would say or call it "loving the hell out of the person"; however, I would just call it "loving the enemy out of the person."

God operates not according to the systems of the world, and for you to realize your calling and the potential that God has given you, means that you have to operate not like you're not of the world. Whereas the world would retaliate using the same tactics that the devil would use: not speaking, turning a deaf ear to the person, talking about them every chance you get, spreading bad things about them. However, this is not the most viable option. Love the enemy out of them, that is the strategy that we must possess. Paraphrasing scripture, God says that "it would heap hot coals upon their heads."

Turn the tides in your favor, if you act as they do you're presenting yourself as no better than they are. So, do it God's way and watch him move on your behalf.

There was a story that I once read that showed us how the enemy was confused when people who were in trouble began to sing songs and call upon the name of the Lord. The story goes on to let us know that as they began to sing songs the enemy became confused. After all, they were supposed to be acting out right now, they were supposed to be very nervous that the enemy was coming in to invade and take away all that they had. The enemy wants you to act like this, he wants you not to re-discover the kingdom's agenda. Re-strategize your plan against the enemy!!!

The same way that you do everything on a daily will yield the same results, and the reason why it would yield the same results is because the enemy gets used to it. Yes, the enemy knows what steps you are going to take next because you did them before. Switch it up, just like the bodybuilder has to switch up the amount of weight that he uses because he doesn't want his muscles to get used to one set of pounds and they get set and stop building up because they are used to the amount of weight to handle. One day they may use more reps and another day they may work on a totally different muscle group. Don't let the enemy get used to you, and how you react to the devil. Set a new trend, and develop a new strategy for dealing with him.

Love the enemy out of the person and love the person back to health. God wants us to be like him representing all that he is and who he is. We can't arrive at this end without nurturing the brother or sister who has become prey for the enemy. Re-strategize, turn the situation around and put it in your favor. This is how you realize your God-given potential. The enemy doesn't want you to love on your enemies but God says if you can't love them, I can't bless you.

It's a hard job but somebody's got to do it. I will be the first to admit that it really takes the love of God living on the inside to even want to look your enemy's way let alone speak to them. Especially after they have done all manner of evil against you, and done things to you it's really hard. However, if we want to be like Jesus, we have to swallow that pill. That pill is a hard piece of medicine to take, but we must be willing to realize that no, this is not about me and all about him.

I remember a story that talked about King David and how he wanted a drink of water from a fountain in Samaria, he stated this to his mighty men and one of the mighty men went over and got this water for him. After he can back and presented this water to David, David poured it out. Why? David poured it out. If they went through all of the obstacles it took just to get that water, he dares not drink it, because in doing so he would have been acknowledging that yes, it is all about me. We must not be afraid to see that , this is not about us all about Jesus and who is in our lives, who he wants us to be.

King David changed his strategy, that's why he was the greatest king that ever lived. He realized that the potential was to serve God, serve Him at all costs. David a man after God's own heart, no he wasn't perfect but God used him mightily when he realized who he was, and who God called him to be. Re-strategize your role against the enemy, and let God fight the major battles in your life, not just the major ones but all of them.

When I was young, the enemy tried all he could to limit my potential, not only did he try to limit my potential, but he tried to take me off earth before it was ever realized. It all started when I was about two years old, I liked to fall asleep while the family went on drives in the country sometimes right there in the town where we lived. On this day, I went to sleep leaning against the door and as the car turned the door came open, and the only thing that was left for me to do was hold on. I want to tell someone that is thinking about giving up that you need to hold on, reach for the door latch and hold on, don't let go.

However, as the story goes I was dragged my knees got some scratches on them but I held on until my father was able to stop the car. The devil tried then but did not succeed. Then calamity later would try to claim my life I got hit by a car and almost lost the potential, however God had invested something in me and He was destined to get a return on the investment. So the enemy tried to take my life again, but God intervened.

I grew older into a man, and the devil was still trying to attack to rob me and God of the potential that is invested in me by the instilling of the heavenly father. However, God would not let it be so. Many times, the enemy has plagued me with the thought of suicide, many times he aggravated me with depressive feelings but God in his wisdom, finds a way to get praise and worship out of the situation.

It's not hard to see what I am suggesting, I am suggesting that I had to strategize. Yes, I had to strategize because undoubtedly the enemy was strategizing his attacks on me. It was certain that I was not going to survive without some type of strategy against the devil, he was not going to get me he was not going to catch me asleep.

In my strategy class, when I was getting my Master's degree we chronicled the strategies of several companies and how they were able to set forth strategies to improve the sales of the company. In the life of Christianity, we must have the same methodology, we must establish strategy to accomplish what it is that God has in us. To develop strategy, we must also develop a Long View take on things. In order to develop lasting change or strategies for unlocking the potential we must see the overall picture. Scripture instructs us that "all things will work together for good to those that love the Lord and are the called according to His purpose" (Rms 8:28). It may not look like it is coming together for us now, but because we have a strategy we know that it will. Jeremiah instructs us that "He knows the thoughts and the plans that He has for us they are for good and not for evil to bring us a future and hope" (Jeremiah 29:11).

Strategy was developed for Wal-Mart and they became one of the leading marketers in the industry of retail. So, we find that it is all about strategy, it is all about finding a means to develop a plan that is going to work for the betterment and one that is going to develop us as an individual. When we are questing to unlock the potential God has given us we have to look at all of the choices that we are presently making because sometimes we make choices based on the things that are presently occurring in our lives. However, God instructs us to meditate on His law both day and night; His plans for us may be different. That is why we must create an open strategy or lead by the will of God.

WEB Dubois stated that" the most important thing to remember in life is that we must never be afraid to leave who we are for the possibility of who we might become" (Dubois, 1961). In saying this when the strategy comes forth we must not be afraid to work the strategy. The Bible suggests that if God is for us He is greater than the world against us, so we must know that the plans that God has for us are good, but we must also strategize to get the totality of our potential. Isaiah instructs us that we must strengthen the stakes, and enlarge the place of our tent construct so in that we see that it requires work, we won't get the things delivered right into our laps we prepare to meet destiny when it comes.

Strategy is everything, strategy determines what services we get. God already has thing laid out for us, he has the map laid out for our destiny we must fill the space with strategy and get to the destiny. God is the navigational system that helps you get there, but your strategy is the mechanism that gives great gains along the way. The bible instructs us that God will be a light unto our feet and a lamp unto our paths, so He in essence illuminates the way.

RE-VERBALIZING

Re-visit what you talk about, re-vamp what you talk about, change who you talk to and also change your conversation as well. When we realize the God-given potential we change our conversation sometimes we must change even who we are conversing too. Scripture instructs us that we must "present our bodies as a living sacrifice holy and acceptable unto God a living sacrifice holy and acceptable unto God who is the reasonable service" (Rms. 12:1). You see in order to change what we verbalize about we must transform our minds in that same passage, we are instructed to renew our minds so that we may prove what is that the perfect and acceptable will of God. Re-verbalizing causes us to talk about the things that God would talk about.

God says we are blessed, He says that we are blessed in the city and in the field, blessed as we come in and as we go; blessed to be the lender and not the borrower so in that we must speak only the things that God suggests that we speak. God says we are blessed, He says that we are prosperous a chosen people, a holy nation and a peculiar people. Verbalize with the right people, in the quest to find the right people we may find that this task is daunting, but I guarantee you it's worth it in the end.

Find people who speak the same words and the same tone as God speaks. God says that you can do all things through Christ that strengthens you, find those people that speak the same. Find those people who constantly make deposits into your life, not those people who constantly make withdrawals. In this life our conversations and those that we converse with is like banking institutions, you see it's either we can make withdrawals or we can make deposits. If we continue to withdraw without replenishing it eventually leaves a negative balance. What we are looking for in this life is positive equity, we are looking for a positive overflow.

Recently, I found myself looking into the purchase of a car I wanted this, and I felt that I couldn't do without it, but in the end, I found that I had a lot of negative equity in the old car that I had as a trade in. What am I saying in this, you won't and never will tap into the destiny that God has for you by always giving, giving, giving and never getting deposited back into it. You will always end up on the negative end. I know that probably sounds selfish to some, but it is God's intention that we become a conduit where the oil of blessing flows out and in the meantime, more flows in.

"Be transformed by the renewing of your mind, that you may prove what is that the good, acceptable and perfect will of the Lord" (Rms 12:1). The key word is renewing, if you are always verbalizing with those who do not allow you to renew your mind the potential that God has placed on the inside of you will never be realized. Be fruitful in your verbalizations, those that you converse with need to be able to deposit a word of encouragement back into you after so many congregants have made withdrawals from you. I serve as an evangelist, and in this life of service, I find it difficult to have those people that are willing to deposit words of encouragement back into me. I've had someone to come up to me in one of my healing and prophetic services and state, "The life of a prophet is a lonely one, I know." Well deposit!!!!!

You will never get to the point where you realize God's potential placed on the inside of you if you verbalize with the same people who aren't willing to deposit back into you. Prayers, encouragement, comfort, etc., are deposits. People feel that I don't hold the office of a prophet etc. therefore, my deposits are necessary. Pray for me that I continue to realize the potential that God has placed in me.

We find in scripture that when God looked for a miracle to take place he changed the atmosphere, he changed those who were around him, he changed those that were in His ear. You can't go to a next-level dimension and get the blessing if you are not willing to change those who are in your ear. When Jesus spoke to Jairus's daughter, the bible says that He went into the room and put them out!!!!! All that remained were the people who were significant to the cause the Mother and Father. What am

I saying, sometimes when we get the next level of blessing, we need to put those who are not significant to the blessing out!! Those who don't believe that the deliverance is going to happen, the bible says put them out!!!!

Change your message, and change who the receptors of the message are. If you go into a place and you are not received wipe the dust from your feet and move on. Someone is willing to hear the message and the impartation that God is speaking. Find those people who speak the same as you, live on the same level as you, and expect the same as you otherwise unlocking your potential will never be realized.

God has dealt with me concerning a lot of things and unlocking the God-given potential happens to be one of them. I don't want to sound like I am trying to separate myself from the world, but if you want the potential to be realized you have to do this. Those who have not suffered with you have no reason to reign with you. Those who didn't know you when you were down in the depths have no reason to be with you when you are in the heights. Not being selfish, but even Jesus, when faced with a question, stated 'are you willing to drink of the same cup that I drink from, are you willing to go through the baptism that I have had to go through." In this life we are always going to find those who want to jump on the cruise boat when everything is in place and the water is calm, but your potential is going to be found in the verbalization that you made when the waters were muddy, when the way was hard.

RE-MOBILIZE

Move from the place where you are standing! Sometimes, the message can't be clearly communicated because you refuse to move from the place where you are standing. Scripture indicates that the gospel message would not have been communicated throughout the world if there was no movement. Sometimes, you need to move from the place where you are standing. I remember a passage of scripture that indicates that Ruth was instructed by Naomi on what to do and when to do it so she could receive the blessing. In essence, she had to move in order to get the blessing, she had to physically change directions to get the blessing.

Sometimes in our lives, not only who we speak to hinders the potential, but where we stand hinders as well. In order to catch the football that the quarterback will throw, the player must transition himself on the field to an area that would allow him to catch the ball. This is the same way in realizing potential; we must sometimes move. We must sometimes get in the way of the blessing.

I remember years ago, the Holy Spirit spoke to me and commissioned me to announce that the quarterback was about to throw and tell the people that it was time to get in the way of the blessing. Sometimes we hinder ourselves because we refuse to get in the way of the blessing, we refuse to move, and we refuse to make a transition in our lives. Sometimes, we are looking for better opportunities to help someone else, and because we refuse to go to the place of blessing the better job is waiting there, the job that would provide the resources for us to be a blessing to someone else. Instead, we just stay where we are, praying for God to bless us when all the time God is saying if you would just move!!!! I have better for you.

Chapter 8
Re-Invest Yourself

Potential can only be realized truly when you re-invest yourself into those things that are important. I can invest all day long but if I invest into things that have no lasting benefits, the potential that I have for making good sound decisions is still not realized. Dr. Roger Parrot, Ph.D., the president of Belhaven University and the author of "The Longview" talks about making decisions as if we are going to be in the position forever. In this he states that the leader, a true leader looks at the real basis of why he is deciding and the decisions that he makes are not for him but for those that are coming after him. That's what Jesus did, he invested in the possibilities that were going to leave a lasting impact on people. He knew that others were going to need healing, saving and sacrifice. So he became the ultimate sacrifice so that we may have a right to the tree of life.

Coming from a lineage like the one Jesus had was far too great to even have to do what he did. However, He said "prepare me a body that I might go down and redeem man.", this was an investment that had great long returns. He invested in something greater than he was. God's family. In unlocking God's potential for us what we invest ourselves in is paramount, what we invest ourselves in determines what we value, and it makes the decision of where we are going. Jesus didn't have too, but in order to make a way for a plethora of people who were going to be born into sin because of Adam and Eve he did.

When we unlock the potential that God has for us through re-investing, we discover a whole new atmosphere, an exciting destiny, a road-trip; if you will. It prioritizes those things that are important to us and to God. For instance, I remember a passage where Jesus was in the Garden of Gethsemane, and while in this garden He was faced with the most treacherous decision, deny the world a savior or cater to His own flesh. He chose to invest himself for the will of God, and choosing to invest Himself created an opportunity for people everywhere to invest themselves in the greater good. This is what I am talking about investing in yourself, the potential that is inside of you was never meant for you if that makes sense.

We must understand that through investing ourselves we should realize that the investment never will really capitalize our opportunities to gloat or look good. It shows maturity, spiritual maturity and that's the potential that we are unlocking. You see God's potential for you, doesn't stop with you. He states in scripture, "I have given you the power to get wealth that I might establish my covenant among the heathen" (Deut. 8:18). So, the promises and the potential is never for us. The blessings that we receive because we realized it will be just incentives to doing it God's way.

You must understand that the totality of the promise was never for you, it's just your duty to unlock the potential to understand the part of story that you play in God's movie. The scripture lets us know in essence that our lives are living epistles that will be read among many, meaning people are going to one day look at how you handle your trials and tribulations and be inspired by them. So you see, that's the potential that we must realize. Yes, I know trials sometimes get the best of us, it seems that you have worked for ever just to find yourself getting nowhere; however still the testimony that you went through will be the book for someone else to read. Handle it wisely!

Live as if you are investing in the future, and that is exactly what it is that you are doing you are investing in the future. The potential is not in your ability to live the life you have always dreamt of, cars, big houses etc., the potential is to realize that the testimony is for someone else, the investing is for someone else. The blessings that will come afterward are just side-effects of the realization of the potential. After you have done the will of the father, you shall receive the promises of the father. Be willing after recognizing what is important invest your time and your mental capacities into that. Nothing that is ever gained wasn't worth investing time into. I know that in this life we invest time into a lot of things and some of those things we never get an adequate return on, this is why we lead a life of prayer; calling on God to help us navigate through this thing that we call life.

LISTEN TO THE ELEVATOR MUSIC

In life no one wants to be entertained by the elevator music, it's usually some dull boring music that plays inside the elevator as you wait to get to the next level or the next floor that you are supposed to be on. It seems like the elevator has gone to the archives of boring music and pulled out an eight-track of the most atrocious music that you ever thought you could hear out. It's boring plus it goes on and on without the hopes of stopping; it seems like it's surrounded by boring after more boring songs that are designed to make you lose your God-given mind. However, be assured that one day it will stop. I don't know how close you will be to losing your mind, but it will definitely stop. Be prepared to dance to the elevator music awhile. What! Do you mean that I have to dance with the fear dance for a while, indefinitely?

Many people in life I have learned, get off of the elevator of life just before the music subsides, just before the pain comes to an end, just before the calls get answered, just before the rescuer comes to rescue you. It is my purpose to let you know that life is going to be hard, but realizing the greatest potential that God has put in you is going to require that you sometimes go through treacherous and boring seemingly meaningless toil. We spoke in other chapters about realizing who you are, and making the strides in knowing the responsibilities that God has placed in you and now that you know who you are here comes the hard part realizing the true potential. The true potential is not that you were made to please you, but you were made to please Him. Sometimes His potential inside of you has nothing to do with you.

We spoke earlier about incentives and side effects, yes blessings and promises of the blessing are things that occur you because you have realized the true potential. So the fine houses, cars, etc. are just side effects of the blessing. The potential that has to be unlocked is indeed not about you, but it's about God's will being performed in you and through you.

Martin Luther King II, Malcolm X, and others all paved the way for us to be able to realize the potential that is in us. However, that potential when adequately realized, is infact not about us at all, but it is about the joy that can be brought to someone else's life through us. If you didn't at all listen to what I was saying about Dr. Roger Parrot, his model is Servant Leadership and he tells us that we must always make decisions as if we are going to stay where we are. In this we probably won't, but it helps us in guiding our hearts to decisions that will bring the best changes for those who are coming behind us. Civil Rights activists' had to go through terrible things just because they had the "Longview", an audacious outlook on how they wanted the world to look for those coming behind them.

Abraham left his kindred and journeyed to a land that God would show him and by doing so his descendants became as numerous as the grains of sand on the seashore, he never got to realize this because it is an ongoing process. However, he was able to unlock his God-given potential. The same with King David, because of one act God said there would never be a person that wouldn't be tied to him left on the throne he didn't live to see it, but it happened, his potential was realized.

The blessing is the after effect, side effect of the potential being realized but the potential is God's plan for others' through you. He said He would bless you if you were obedient to His plan. In paraphrasing scripture only until after you have exercised the will of the father, shall you partake in the promises of the father. Once we stop clouding our minds with the potential being about us, and discover that it is more about Him than it is us we can make strides in unlocking it.

DANCING WHILE INVESTING

Just like the investor who invests in that big strip mall takes joy in the investing portion because he knows that once it's up and running and stores start leasing compartments and all that rental income starts to come in it's a big return; we must do the same. We rejoice because we are finally realizing what God has placed us here for, we dance because we are finally making it happen for others. This is truly dancing. If we can only dance when good things are happening for us, when our career is being propelled forth, then my friends I am sad to report that the potential God wants has yet to be realized.

I'm talking about that speech at Mason's temple in 1968 where an exuberant MLK stated that 'I might not get there with you but I have seen the mountain top" exuberant about the joy of knowing that others' would ultimately get there, not knowing that his fate would be forever sealed the next day, he still was able to celebrate the fact that somebody else would not have to grow up in an atmosphere like the one he knew. That is what realizing the God-given potential is.

Living out of obedience and not sacrifice. I am talking about the negative sacrifice. However, living and unlocking the God-given potential is a life of sacrifice, can we imaging sacrificing so others' can have and we never realize those things? Can we imagine fulfilling God's purpose and plan and thereby becoming the "guinea pig" if you will for the pleasures of God. This is what realizing the plan and unlocking the God given potential is.

People who remained exuberant about what God was doing through them, Abraham, I am certain did not want to partake in the sacrificing of his only son a son that he and his wife had prayed earnestly for, but he realized something greater than he. He realized that the action of obedience was greater, and because of his one act of faith, set forth a chain of events of faith he became the father of faith. He was able to celebrate in realizing that God-given potential, he became one who was registered in the hall of faith believers. Once we realize that the potential is not about us but about Him, then all other things fall in place. As scripture instructs us "Seek ye first the kingdom of God and all of these other things shall be added to you" (Matt. 6:33). We have to understand the total message of that, God is not telling us to seek the things but seek the potential of the kingdom and once we are obedient enough to seek the potential of the kingdom, he would bless the things that we are needing. For instance, in Philippians 4:19 it is declared, "My God shall supply all of your needs according to His riches that are in Glory" this is only after we have helped someone else by realizing the potential in us as being called to Christianity. So you see the God-given potential has never been about us, it's about realizing what God wants and desires to do for the world through us.

Chapter 9
Releasing Inadequacy

Scripture tells us that we are created in the image of our Lord and Savior Jesus Christ, it says that we were created in His likeness. In His image He made us, formed us from nothing into something therefore there should be no sign of turning within us. There should be no timidity within us. However, living in a society that wants or desires to measure us according to its standards can create a sub-standard view of who we are. Unfortunately, it becomes certain that we will never realize who we are or even the potential that God has instilled in us. Looking at oneself as nothing becomes easy for people to partake in feelings of self-pity, and sometimes self-degradation. Not measuring up to people. We should often stop and ask ourselves who gave the one the measuring stick that he or she is holding? Did God? Did society? No one can measure your standards but God he is the only measuring stick or person you should be measuring yourself by.

There was a woman in the Bible, Zarephath in the book of Kings to be exact. She used the measurement of society to measure what she could and could not be or do. She held herself in everybody else's picture frame, the frame that society created for her was a frame that she tried to fit into, but unfortunately didn't have the means to fit in the frame. We as humans, we often find ourselves trying to fit into a frame of society, we try to lose weight in order to fit, we try to gain weight in order to fit, we try to have surgery to correct everything about us that we feel is wrong in order to fit. We never end up fitting, we never end up achieving the end that we want to see.

You may be asking what am I talking about in this, you see the mother made a choice for her son, she said that my son and I will eat the cake and we are going to die. The son did not request to die, he did not even display any signs that he wanted to get rid of his life. He might have wanted to live a little longer, he may have wanted to see what God could do for them. Afterall, he was a young child why should he cut off his life at such a early age? Why should he even want to become a statistic? Why should he not want to give life a try? My point is society makes choices for us all the time, society tries to make decisions for us constantly. This is my point. Your potential will never be realized if we continue to let society put us in a frame. Allowing society to place you in a frame, or vindict what it is that you do even the choices you make, allows for inadequacies, they allow for chances as well as opportunities for persons to feel that they are inadequate. This is because the choice was made for them and they were not allowed to make that decision themselves.

When choices are made for us, we place ourselves in a mindset that says "the box is not worth opening" I have no reason to explore higher heights and deeper depths in Christ. From the beginning of time, choices were allowed to made by individual people, take Adam and Eve for instance, they were allowed to make the choice to eat the fruit, even though they knew what the consequences were.

Inadequacies touch us all in different ways, inadequacies have different aspects of our lives that it seems like they enjoy to capitalize on. Inadequacies are something that will always be plagues in our lives and they will always try to attach themselves to us and ruin any relationship that we might start with anyone notably Jesus. This is what the devil likes to see happen in our lives, if he can ruin our potential by placing the inadequacies on us, he feels great; if he can ruin the dreams and visions that we have about how the future will be for us, he enjoys it. Scripture states, "For I know the thoughts and plans that I have for you saith the Lord, plans to prosper you give you a future and a hope," Jer 29:11. This becomes more and more foggy when it becomes attached to the devil-driven inadequacies, it become a scenario in which you are asking "Where is God, and what is His role in this that is happening to me?"

Inadequacies make us feel this way toward the current situations that are going on in our lives, inadequacies don't allow you to see the blessings that God has already provided, inadequacies limit your view to what is going on at that time in your life. God has potential that needs to be worked out in you, and the possibility of thwarting that becomes prevalent when inadequacies present themselves. Inadequacies are real and they can provoke depression and thoughts of suicide, it drains you from the power that you should know and realize that God has given you. You actually don't have the power to rebuke it, you don't have the power to speak the word over your life, you don't have the happiness in your life that you know a child of God should be experiencing.

I know what this is, but the spirit of God would like you to know that there is a releasing of the inadequacy; you have to release the inadequacy to realize the potential that you were created to accomplish. You see every human being that God has ever designed has a unique piece of the puzzle of His plan to accomplish, and the devil's job is to create a stumbling block in your way. Why? he figures that God is too powerful to get back at Him for expelling him from Heaven, so he targets the children who are His heirs. He tries to block the future, the dreams, the hopes, the aspirations and he tries this through depression, inadequacies and a lot of other things. The job of the saint is to praise Him (God) in spite of the turmoil going on. The job is to be a beacon in the dark that the enemy is trying to create in the lives of the direct heirs of Christ.

Many years ago, there was book written and in this book, it chronicled the life of Dr. Martin Luther King, it also chronicled the livelihood of the Civil Rights movement. The title of the book was "Why we can't wait." it talked about the tactics that were so often times put in place to block any progress toward the chosen potential of the Civil Rights movement. It documented the Plessy v. Ferguson separate but equal declaration and how it was overturned by Brown v. Board of Education with the famed justice Thurgood Marshall and how the turnout was that separate but equal was declared unconstitutional and schools were ordered to integrate with all deliberate speed. It chronicled how in August 1961 that would be derailed by the passage of the Pupil Placement Law. This, my brothers and sisters are what the devil decides to do, he wants to derail the purpose of the creation that God has in us.

Releasing the inadequacy is what God wants us to do, I admit it's hard. I had several things that I battled with, mornings that I would wake up and through that night I would wrestle with the devil and wake up with the inadequacies on my mind. I wake up mad with the world, mad about what I thought I should have and don't, mad about not receiving the promises when I thought I should receive them, mad about my age my status in life, and my progress. This is what the enemy desires to do, he wages war while you are sleep and tries to prepare your mind so you won't be thankful on the next day. I resent the tactics that the enemy use and you should too. Release the inadequacy so we can access the potential that God has in us.

We can't wait because the enemy wants to cause you to go a wall and jeopardize all of the potentials that he has placed inside of you. We can't wait because God is not in the business of not receiving a return on His investment.

My inadequacy was deep it always affected me, it affected me and ultimately would try to block me from reaching any potential that God would have for me. Every morning, every evening, the same dilemma was ever-present before me, I would ask God for His help and His hand in my life; however, the problem was I wasn't able to wait for His strong deliverance. The potential must be realized, the potential must be realized and in order for it to be realized it the inadequacies must be released.

God has designed all of us to meet a designated potential and a design for our lives, turmoil and inadequacies come to break that up but our potential must be greater. Yes, there are times that we all want to give up because of the challenges of our inadequacies and the things that they place in our lives, but we can't give up, we can't quit, and we must change the mentality the paradigm that we have or what our inadequacies have placed us in. It's hard I understand, and I want you to understand, but yes, you can overcome it; you may have scares from those psychological battles, but you will overcome and realize the potential.

We all may face inadequacies, inadequacies in our finances, inadequacies in our marriages, and sometimes inadequacies in who we are and who we were created to be. However, God has instructed all of us that we were created in His own image in the image of Him, He created us. God has designed all of us with the power to overcome those inadequacies and discover our true potential, which is actually His potential. The reason I say that it is actually His potential is because Paul tells us in Hebrews that after we have done the will of the father, we should receive the promises of the father, which lets us know that it is not our potential but His potential. Deuteronomy 8:18 tells us that "We should know the Lord thy God for it is He who gives us the power to get wealth, that He might establish His covenant among the heathen." So, in this we find that it is actually His potential that we are realizing, the fact that He has already created us in His own image to accomplish His purposes.

In Ezekiel chap. 36 God instructs us that He is going to switch things around for His people; however, He will not do it because of our name or for our own ability to shine; however, He is going to do it for His own name the name that the heathen profane, the name that the heathen take out of context and say that God can't do a thing. God says He is going to correct that; the heathen won't be able to go around saying that "you are serving a God who is not able to take care of His people" but rather He says that the scoffer will no longer be able to scoff at your famine. He says that the name of the heathen profane in the earth will be made great again, He will not suffer the scoffer to be in a position to say that the people of God have a father who is not acquainted with what servants of His are going through.

So in this, we see that it is actually God's potential and not that of ours, our potential is the potential that God wants to be realized in us, we are children of God, so as a result, if we are created to be like Him, then the potential that we realize is the potential that is to be reflective of God. God initiated this in the beginning of the world and furthermore let us know in scripture He says that we may show the glory of the one who has called us out of the darkness, into the marvelous light, and no one but God has done that! No one else could do it for us, but a sovereign Lord and an all-knowing God.

When we realize that the potential that we are actually trying to reach is that of God, the way will be made much clearer for us. When the reality of the potential is shown, then we will stop trying to fit in where God didn't design us to fit. We are intricate pieces of a puzzle and we are not designed to fit everywhere, but in the loyalties of life we attempt too; if we can see that God is trying to maximize our potential in other areas, then we would be open to where He leads and directs us. After all, it is His potential that we want accomplished in the earth realm. When we totally sell ourselves out to Him, His vision becomes our vision, His wants become our wants, so we begin to ask to be close to Him we indirectly ask for Him to be our reality. We begin to ask what it is that He wants us to do, how can we satisfy His need to fulfill His covenant, we realize that the potential was His in the beginning.

God is nigh to us more than we can ever truly make Focus on. He is there to help us fulfill the potential that He has designed for us.

Paul was an apostle of Christ, and in the 8 Chapter of Acts about the 28 verse, He is prized for asserting these words "And we know that all things work together for the God to them that love the Lord and those who are called according to His purposes." So, we see in this scripture that it was His potential from the very beginning, this was over 2000 years ago, it was not just written. His purposes, you see, once we start to love the Lord as the scripture and commandments instruct us, then everything that happens in our life is for the good, because we love the Lord and innately aids us in accomplishing His purposes. It is His potential that we are realizing. I know that this reading is entitled "Unlocking you God-given Potential," but we must understand that each plan that God has for us is a part of His potential, He uses us in different ways to paint His big picture. It is like God is the painter and we are the models for that picture, one serves as the color green for grass, one may serve as the yellow for the sun, one may serve as the color blue for the sky; however, we all serve in His picture. That is why the scripture declares that we are the craftmanship of God. Because we are who He uses us to accomplish His purposes.

To better understand the potential that is within us, we are to develop a closer relationship with the father, we are able to develop a relationship with God so that we may learn His ways, and meditate upon His precepts. I am reminded of a story in the scripture, the story involves a man who went to Jesus by night, to learn how to be born again. For years and years people have concentrated on the fact that he came to Jesus by night, why night in the day where everyone could see, why not among all of the other on lookers why hide out at night? It has become my analysis that in seeking out an honest relationship, you don't want to be disturbed by the glim and glamour of everything around you,. when you have your Focus on everything around you , you fail to get the message, you fail to realize the purpose of the teaching. My take was the man in John 3 came to Jesus by night in order to get a proper relationship with Christ,. many others need to really come to Him by night, so we don't get caught up in the feeling of being super-saved and seek to gain publicity rather the intimacy that comes with a right relationship with God. God calls us to be intimate with Him thus we can discover the Kingdom's Agenda and not that of our own. Properly discovering and unlocking the God-giving potential.

So the Bible says that He came to Jesus by night, anxious to learn the ways of Christ, he was so anxious about learning the ways of Christ and it was such a desire of his that we was willing to forsake everything. Had the Pharisees caught him associating with a blasphemer it would have been detrimental. After all he would have openly gone against his own sect, he would have been in total defiance of the rule at that time. He was so anxious to learn these ways that he was willing to undergo what could have been sudden death.

Nicodemus was this man's name. We have so many Nicodemus's in the church today, by that I mean those in the church that want that closer relationship with the true God, they want to experience the realness of disciple ship; however, because of the Pharisees that are present in the church and the world today they don't gain the pleasure of securing a relationship. Becoming a destined but undesired fate of not knowing Him in the way they want too. Realizing the God-given potential, we must be willing to let God orchestrate our lives, for it is no longer ours but His to live through us. Challenging ourselves to come to Jesus by night is notably not the most desirable thing to do, but it is worthwhile. It promotes us and puts in a place to really realize what God's potential is, His potential is His desires for us; and as I stated before once we get in Him our desires become His desires.

The 17 Chapter of the book of Proverbs states "A man who follows wise company, he becomes wise." The potential for us to become what God has designed for us is determined by those that we follow, the scripture states that those who are led by the spirit are the sons of God. So you see if we are following God, as scripture dictates then it is inevitable that we become the potential that God wants us to achieve. The aforestated scripture states "A man who follows wise company, he himself becomes wise." Those that are wise follow after the things of God and those that don't follow the wise things of God, don't reach the potential that God has for them.

"After that the spirit has come upon you, you shall be witnesses unto me in Judaea, Samaria and the utmost parts of the earth." It is when we realize the potential that God wants us to live, that we no longer accept the marginalization of our witness. We no longer accept the opinions of people who say that we can only witness to this or that sect of people, but we have become witnesses unto God and not unto a denomination, not unto a religion. Religion is based from the base word "ritual" it is something that you do repeatedly and it is not necessarily a form of Christianity. Christianity is a belief in which we become followers of Christ., religiosity is a belief in which we become followers of a religion. The potential that God has for us will never be found living under the marginalization of a denomination or any man's rules. If we learn to abide by God's rules and not made-man doctrine then the potential can become realized. The scripture states that if anyone is to come unto you preaching any gospel other than this gospel let him have the spirit of the anti-Christ. We have to know that the potential lies in our ability to develop a closeness, relationship if you will with Christ. We can't know the potential that He wants or even has for us unless we get into the instruction manual, "the bible."

BEING BETTER, NOT BITTER

When we are in the quest to capitalize and discover our God-given potential, we have to learn that every experience that we go through is to make us stronger, fierce, resilient, develop our backbone and to give us roots. Naomi and Ruth are a prime example of this; they could have chosen to become bitter over the situation both lost their husbands, the other daughter-in-law Orpah left them after her husband died; Ruth chose to stay with Naomi. That whole situation could have become catastrophic, they didn't have a kinsmen redeemer, no one to provide for them, no one to help them but instead of "bailing" on each other they stayed together until God changed the situation. When we are discovering our true potential, we must hang tough until God changes the situation. I imagine looking at each other saying we have nothing to eat tonight, we have nowhere to sleep tonight, what person is going to let us borrow some money or sleep in one of their rooms tonight all of these questions undoubtedly, I can imagine going through their heads if it were in today's time it would have been very dis-hardening. But Ruth became better, she became better in the aspect that she was willing to receive direction from Naomi on how to be led to the blessing. We have to be willing sometimes to be lead or given direction on how to achieve the potential that God has for us. She became better from everything she went through. We know the continuation of that story, about how she uncovered

Boaz's feet and put the cover over her at the bottom of the bed, and at midnight the bible records that he turned over and saw her there. The potential that God designed for her to have and be able to access was discovered.

Naomi told her to go wash her face, perfume herself and go where he was. Sometimes to access the potential we must wash our faces of all of the bad things that we have encountered in life, we must anoint our faces with the anointing that breaks the yoke, we must forget about the things that were done to us for today is a new day, yesterday was and now it is gone, the hurt is now gone, the constant agony of not thinking that you were ever good enough is gone, despite of what people tell you and try to make you believe it's gone, it's all gone. She says to perfume yourself put on that screen that makes you smell good to God, makes your fragrance go before him as a sweet-smelling savor, that perfume is the alms that God is waiting to see go before him, that perfume is the prayers that God is longing for you to pray, that perfume is the blood that God is waiting for you to cover yourself with, that perfume is the aroma that God is wanting you to smell like telling you to come home, I am waiting for you to give you a future and a hope. I love you with an everlasting love. The perfume is the meditation that God desires to have with you. That perfume is the potential that he has bottled inside you. Paraphrased, we have these treasures in an earthen vessel. Be good and be blessed in Jesus' name.

She tells her to go to the place, sometimes discovering our God-given Potential may lead us to some rocky places, stony places, places that are destined to destroy us it appears. God says don't count it out that this is the place to discover your potential. Go to the place, we must get ready to be present, be effective where we are going and be active. God says that the steps of a good man are ordered by the Lord, you can't make a wrong step if God is ordering those steps. So go to the place, you'll discover potential waiting when you get there. You will discover peace when you get there. Be not afraid with fear and uncertainty about where He is leading you and what he is doing in your life, go to the place.

Becoming the Frame

It is recorded in the book of Kings that there was a widow woman who wasn't living the good life, so-to-speak, she and her son was in the house at a time when famine was in the land. The Bible records that she met a Man of God by the name of Elijah, the Bible states that this man asked her to make him a cake. Can you imagine someone being so selfish as to ask you to do something for them eventhough they see that you are already struggling, already trying to fight for food, already looking through bare cabinets trying to find something to eat, trying to navigate through an empty cabinet, looking at pots with dust in them, looking at a garden with dry plants, looking at the ground that was not capable of producing any fruit, looking at the ground that has already cracked because the famine was making the land dry and barren, looking at corn stalks where corn used to be but the crows already ate. Looking at the okra that has dried up because there is no water to saturate them. The story goes on to let us know that the Man of God asked the woman to bake him a cake. He first asked what she was planning to do, she stated that she was going to bake a cake for her and her son they were going to eat and they were going to die. She didn't bother to see if her son wanted to see what the plans of God was for his individual life, she didn't bother to see if he wanted to hold on a little longer and see whether the promises of God were going to work for him. She didn't ask him what he wanted to do, but she made the choice for him, she stated what she thought that he wanted to do, she made a choice for him.

We must see in life that there will be people who try to make the choices for us, they try to force us to do something that we don't want to do, they try to make us live out in a sign that we don't want to live in, but we are our own people a people who are free to choose and if we are to fulfill the potential we must choose God. Once we choose him, then our strength bursts forth speedily, our heaviness is lifted, our weights are made lighter because we begin to have confidence in the things that he provides us and we begin to see the potential the God-given potential come out, his desires, his plans for our lives, we begin to unlock the God-given potential. It is funny how the God-given potential that we seek is actually the potential of God. We can never obtain a potential that is that of our own, because the reality in ourselves is the person that we are trying to get away from. We are trying to become more like him. So, it is the potential of God that we are trying to unlock.

God is the source that is in the resource, so he is in control of the God-given potential that we seek. He is the reality of the potential that we possess. We must be so aware that society doesn't make the choices for us, as to what potential we possess. As the story about the widow woman goes on, she suggests that her son and she was going to eat the cake and that they we going to die. God's potential says that he is the author and the finisher of the faith and by the scripture saying that he is the author and the finisher of our faith says that he starts it, he is in the middle of it, and he concludes it and that is the same thing with the potential that we seek. He starts it, he maintains it, and he finishes it.

Believe in the potential that you have in yourself, God has made you wonderful and he has fearfully made you; so live your life always expecting God to show up in your life. God has potential in you, and for you, we just need to be able to tap into it and allow God to exhibit all the gifts that he has given us in our life. To understand the will of God for your life is a gift and a present that only you can unwrap, you have to be willing to do the work and do the exploration that it takes to unwrap the gift that God has gifted you as an individual. Praises to God for the things that He does in the lives of His people; in giving them the tools that they need as they navigate through this thing that we call life and it would be a blessing if we possibly find the God-given potential along the way.

When we wholeheartedly trust God, as the woman eventually did we can realize that what was what we thought would hurt us, eventually blesses us and allows us to realize our potential.

Chapter 10
Releasing Negative Energies

Finding our God Given Potential, we must discover that we must release the negative energies, not only our negative energies but we must get away from the ones who find it hard not to share their negative energies. I mean, have you ever heard of people who talk you out of something that God was telling you to do for someone else? Have you ever encountered people who can tell you a whole run down on other people and make you change your mind about what you thought to do for them? People are so toxic that they can never forget anything that the person has ever done to them that might have been wrong. People who can't let the past go. People who sabotage their own future because of the outlook that they will not change. God says that you have to rid yourself of that negative energy, you have to find positive people, people who are not constantly re-hashing what was wrong and what was and really is not anymore. We must discover that God wants and desires us to go higher in His promises and if we hold onto negativity, that will never happen for us. When we hold onto what should have been, what could have been, what we could have do if so-so would not have stopped me. It reminds me of a story of a man who desired to be whole. However, he was riddled with excuses.

There was a man by the pool of Bethsaida desiring to be whole, he encountered Jesus and Jesus offered him the opportunity to be whole, the man offered every excuse in his philosophical book of excuses that is, he stated that every-time he steps to the pool when the water is troubled someone steps in front of him and thus pushes him out of the way. Some people just would rather the status quo, they would rather things remain the way they are, if they are made rid of the situation that they are dealing with, they would have nothing to talk about. They have literally fell in love with their story, the story has become so dramatic for them they love telling it and they don't want to be healed from it so they continue to offer excuses to provide the reasons that they still linger where they are. That was this man, God himself offered the opportunity to be healed, to be whole to no longer have a reason to go back to being negative, a reason to no longer lay in self- pity, to no longer have a pity party, to no longer indulge in a reason to create debacles in life. However, some people don't want that to change. They continue to use negativity as a force field to hold or as an excuse not to realize the God Given potential.

Releasing the negative energy and discovering your God Given potential requires patience, it requires a life of boldness. The reason it requires a life of boldness is that if you have been around negativity almost all of your life you have become accustomed to negativity, you have become one with the negativity that you have heard so you must disconnect yourself from those people you must disconnect yourself from those situations that have caused you to start to look at things through negative lenses as well. It is hard and I understand that, but in order to develop a mindset that will be willing to walk into God Given potential, you must be willing to launch out in the deep and do something different. There is a saying that says if you want to experience something different you must do something different and that it is insanity to do the same thing every day and expect different results. Don't fall in love with your story if you fall in love with your story, you will never see the need to change it. As stated before you co-author you destiny. God is the author and the finisher of your faith but you co-author it, you determine what choices that are to be made. You mustn't forget your story, however you shouldn't fall in love with it either. Your story shapes you for the potential that God allows you to walk into, on the other hand falling in love with blocks you from walking into God Given potential.

As I stated before Ruth had every opportunity to fall in love with her story, she could have chosen to say woe is me, my husband has died and I don't have the kinsman redeemer that would take care of me. Further, my mother-in-law's husband has died I might as well sit here and die. Still, she didn't choose too she chose not to fall in love with her story. Still, she became a builder, she became a laborer, she became someone who would take ownership of the outcome of her own destiny. In this story we should take ownership of our own story instead of falling in love with the story. We see that as she began to work towards a positive end, she became the great-great grandmother of our Lord and Savior Jesus Christ. The destiny was changed all because of that one act of faith, she said that she would follow her mother-in-law and her people would become her people. Your story shapes the potential that you inherit, your story paves the road that the car called potentially drives on. Don't fall in love with your story, it would make you abort the potential that God has for you, it would make you forsake the opportunities that God has for you. Be an inventor a game-changer, don't get stuck with the story that life deals to you, re-invent your story, you have the pin re-write it.

When we release negative energies more than just getting away from those situations and people in our lives that allow us to embrace those negative energies; we sometimes must remember those concepts that we used to think about in positivity. What practices that we used to allow to operate in our lives we sometimes need to know those again. The Bible lets us know in the 4 chapters of Genesis after Cain killed Abel and was banished to the land of Nod. Adam and Eve basically lost out on two sons, Abel the fruitful one, was dead the one whose offering was acceptable to God, the one who thought about what he was offering to God, the one who didn't tithe out of religion, the one who was thoughtful about his gifting to God. Since Cain killed him, that son was lost, then God intervened and banished Cain so that son was lost as a result of that one act. So Adam and Eve the parents had no more children. However, the Bible says something that will forever permeate the psyche of Christendom, that will forever create a constructive question in the mind of theologians. It says that Adam knew Eve again, it says that once he knew her, she conceived a son and named him Seth; it goes on to tell us that Seth had a son called Enos, and then man began to invoke the name of the Lord.

It is important to note, that before that one act of knowing the lineage of every person in the Bible would be traced back to sin, however that one act changed the face of biblical history, and man began to invoke the name of the Lord. It lets us know that whatever we think our story is, whatever debacle we think we have gotten ourselves in God says that if we can just begin to know peace again, know joy again, know tranquility again, know the blood again, know faith again we can change what is going on in our lives we can re-vamp the roller-coaster that we call our lives. God wants us to live as to unlock the God Given potential that is on the inside of us.

I want you to know that God is telling you today that your Seth has come, your key to your future has come, the story has changed you have the pen to continue writing your story. There's glory after this!

In releasing negative energies, it is often found that it will not be an easy task at all, we were taught negativity from birth. We were taught to cry when we wanted something, even if we weren't hungry or bored but it was just because we wanted it. We were taught to say who was ugly and who was pretty, I mean who defines what those actually are. We were taught to call people fat, skinny, tall or short. All those are negative connotations, and we thus find in our lives that society put us in those categories. Shows on television tells us that in order to be the top model we have to be a certain size, plus size category gay or straight, bi-sexual or curious those are negative energies. God designates who we are not society. People have contemplated suicide because of negative energies, people have committed suicide because of negative energies. If we don't get anything else from life, we should know that God has made us and when he made us we were fearfully and wonderfully made in His likeness. Not anyone else's.

I am reminded of a story in the Bible that tells us that there was a widow woman who had four sons, bills and a husband who had died, which is a bad combination. This woman had creditors to come to get her sons because of debts she owed. She consulted the man of God as the bible states and the Man of God told her what to do, He said go borrow some vessels and get not a few, pour oil in each one of the vessels until the oil fills them up. The widow proceeded to do what she was told, she got vessels and began to pour oil, the scripture says as long as there were vessels there was oil, but when the vessels ran out the oil stayed. It lets us know that once you opt to follow society and not God's plan for your life you will always run out of resources but when you are obedient to His plan you will have overflow.

As the story goes, she poured the last bit into the last vessel and it was enough to pay all of her debts. When we follow the plan of man, the plan that told the lady that the vessels she had gotten was enough, the plan that told her that she didn't want to look greedy, the plan that innately and indirectly didn't want her to believe what the Man of God had told her, if she didn't rely on man's plan but the plan of God she would've been in overflow, but instead she could only live until it was gone.

That's the problem we are so busy trying to live up to and fulfill man's expectations that there is no room for us to allow God's plan to take place in our lives. God through Elijah had a plan for her to live in abundance for the rest of her life, but she didn't get enough vessels. All of that my friends is negativity------and what is negativity, it is the refusal to follow your God's path but follow your own path. Jeremiah 29:11 says I know the plans that I have for you thus saith the Lord plans to prosper you to give you hope and future plans for your good. However, living in the negativity of onlookers we doubt it.; I am here to make sure you release the negativity.

Chapter 11
The Winner in Me

We all must realize that there is a winner in every one of us. God created us that way and it is only until we follow the steps outlined in this book that we step into that realization. We must re-align ourselves with God-given, God-instructed words that are designed to put us in the proper place with him and where He wants us to be. I am reminded of a story of a prophet by the name of Elisah, this prophet had seen many things wrought by God in his life but yet when it came down to one little woman, he denied the presence of the winner inside. The Bible instructs us that he was startled when she told him that because he through God's power slew the prophets of Baal; she would make his life like one of them, he ran. The Bible records that he ran and ran, did he not only run, but he ran away from the presence of God. Life in the course of his running found him in a cave on Mt. Moab, this is where he heard several things. He heard lightening, he heard thunder, he heard different things, the Bible records that it was not until he heard the still same voice in that of a whisper, it was God's voice. This lets us know that you have to be able to be knowledgeable when God is speaking, he will not be in the extravagance of everyday life, nor the glamour of the high-end things that we think He would dwell in. However, lowly He came, lowly He will speak. The Bible records that the voice asked Elisah what was he there for, along with several other questions. It records that after all of the questions, the voice instructed him to go an anoint someone else for the journey.

The voice would stick with Elisah throughout the journey, guiding him. You would ask "why would a voice guide him, even though he was running away from the presence of that voice?' This is where we have to identify the true character of God, God is a God who doesn't guide you away from his presence; if you choose not to identify that there is a winner in you, He is a God of compassion, he nurtures you all because He loves and respects your choices. He is a God who is willing to give you rest when your journey has become too much for you. We see in this passage that the voice (angel of the Lord) also instructed Elisah to go and lay under the juniper tree, instructed him to eat for the journey was too much for him. God showed him compassion, this was the same man who had walked in the footsteps of a worthy follow-ship of Elijha, the same man whose mantle he had gotten. This was the same man who raised a woman's son, the same man who prayed and God shut the heavens so that there would be no rain. Same man who had earlier seen his instructor taken to heaven in whirlwind. The same man who spearheaded the school of the prophets, and cause an ax head to float on top of water. The same man who found life in pot of cursed and poisoned stew, now afraid and tired. God recognized this and is now giving him the opportunity to rest and giving him help for the journey.

We must identify the winner in us, God has put the winner in us but he also identifies with us when we are tired and have fought our course and made a good run. That doesn't mean that Elisah was a loser by any means, sometimes winning is knowing when to pass the baton to someone else, sometimes winning is knowing when you have run the last mile that you can. Sometimes winning is knowing when it's time to let someone take the helm. We all have the tools that are necessary for us to live a victorious life, however, we must acknowledge that there is a winner is us. We win, this situation….we win this saga……we win this circumstance……..God has created us to win. We win!

Jeremiah 29:11 says" I know the thoughts and the plans that I have for you plans to prosper you, plans to prosper you not to harm you to give you a future and a hope, and an expected end." No matter what you are going through right now, no matter what you are faced with there is an expected end, and we expect victory every-time. No matter what we face in life, we are designed to have victory. Isaiah says it best He says that "No weapon that is formed against us, shall prosper and every tongue that exalts itself in judgment shall be utterly condemned for this is the heritage of the servants of the Lord and the payback is of me saith the Lord. It's in our bloodline and lineage to be healed, blessed and delivered.

The biggest enemy or opposition in being able to identify the winner in us is the reflection of us. We sometimes involve ourselves with things that don't give us a clear view of who we are, and it derails our vision of knowing that the winner is inside of us. This is why God wants us to see the reality, this is why He says that we are fearfully and wonderfully made, because He wants us to identify with who He made us to be, who He purposed for us to become. He wouldn't have warranted us to become it, if He knew that He didn't give us the tools to make it. So, this is why He created us with it already inscribed in our DNA. Every good thing comes from the Lord above, all of the tools that we have pertain to life and health, the health of our bodies, the health of our souls, the health of our spirits and the health of our emotions. When we overcome the things that are blocking us from realizing the winner, we will annihilate the opposition that shows up in our lives so often just to show it's ugly head. There is a winner in you, however the object of what it is that you need to find yourself doing is finding the "twin flame" in your life the twin flame that drives you into your purpose, the flame that pushes you to be better; when you connect with that individual or muse or whatever it is then you find yourself nudging into your potential. You find yourself finding out what the true purpose of your life is. Elisah found his "twin flame" in the person of Elijah, and Joshua found his "twin flame" in the person of Moses who pushed him into destiny or some would say the next dimension. Finding your "twin flame" is hard to do but when you accomplish this the task of discovering your potential is easier. Timothy found the "twin flame" in Paul and the list goes on; my point is find that person who catapults you into greater, propels you into challenges, promotes you to try and be better at doing things, the person who doesn't always say "yes" the person who critiques you all of the time. The person who criticizes you not destructive but constructive. The person who constantly gets under your skin. The person who makes you uncomfortable, the person who challenges everything you do and say. The person who suggests improvements in you. Holds you accountable to things you say, and then reminds you of it when you don't do come through.

The twin flame is someone that can stand with you not when you are on top of the mountain, but can stand with you when you're down in the valley. To us, a lot of us that person is Jesus, however society and the "powers" have strategically placed those individuals on earth for us. There are here for our perfection, the perfecting of the saints.

Martha and Mary were two sisters who encouraged each other, served as "twin flames" for each other we are to do the same for our brothers and our sisters on this earth. God has given each of us this assignment, and what is the assignment that we "Love one another."

The good thing about "twin flames" is no matter who you are, where you are from, or what religious beliefs you have it all boils down to the fact that you must find your "twin flame." No, we won't delve into which religion is the right one, nor which way is the correct way to worship God. Whether your belief is in Budha, Mohammed, or any other of these you need to find the straight path and walk therein. You are you and I am me, so your "twin flame," however that may look needs to be found. As for me I make my affirmation in this book, the one true God for me is God. Jehovah Elohim, Elshaddai, Rohe, Raja, Rapha., He is God.

A 'twin flame" is one of those contemporaries that can think the same thoughts at the exact same time finish the sentence that you started out saying. Yes, I know you're thinking that sounds like a marriage; in a way it is. A marriage of thoughts, a marriage of beliefs, a marriage of concepts, a marriage of a way of life. If you haven't found the "twin flame" yet I suggest you do so. It will help in your navigation into "finding the potential God has created you for". Paul and Silas the Bible tells the story that they were locked in jail for praising their God-----but. The story goes on to share with us that through

Their witness guards where saved and the Bible declares that at midnight chains started to break off the prison doors. This is what "twin flames" can do, when you have a connection of thoughts, a connection of beliefs, both believing the same thing and their mind is on the same thing. There is nothing that can't be realized when this occurs. God wants us all to walk into this reality. However, the choice is yours.

Chapter 12
The Leading, The Lesson and the Learning

How many of you have ever wondered why you feel like you were led into something that had no benefit whatsoever. It seemed like you were just in an existence of nothing- ness, an existence that seemed like it had no purpose for your life, and after all that's what we are here for, we are here to find the true purpose of our existence we are here to explore how we can serve others' while serving God and fulfill the purpose that we were placed here for. However, we go through things that seemingly have no real true purpose or no meaning to the reasons that we feel we were placed here for; it seems like a derailment or detour. Why can't the true meaning for our experiences just be told to us? Why can't they the role in my life be explained? Why not just give the true meaning? Why do we have to navigate through our lives and find out the reason of our existence? Well, if you're like me, you often wonder why you go through different stuff just to end up like you have moved nowhere like you are riding in a vehicle that can only go four miles per hour and it takes forever for you to get to the place that destiny promises to be waiting. Well, I'm sure that Jesus felt the same way being led into the wilderness by the spirit, having to be tempted by the adversary himself. One would ask why He just come out of fasting, which is something that seemingly was a positive thing, just to be led into the wilderness by the spirit of God.,why? What was the purpose in that? What was He supposed to learn in that? What was the reason that was behind the whole experience?

Sometimes we as people following after God, have to wonder this. We are left to wonder why is God allowing us to go through something that seemingly have no purpose? Something that seemingly is like that automobile that has a speedometer that will only go pass three miles per hour. It seems like we have gone through several detours and so many setbacks that it seems that we will never make it to the sense of it all. Well, these experiences and these problems exists with us all. It doesn't provide much encouragement for us. However, I need you to know that there is a lesson in the leading, there is a learning in the leading. God does not lead us into situations unless there is a learning for us to take out of it. He does not allow us to go through experiences unless there is a purpose in it that we are supposed to learn. Many times, we are all faced with situations that we are to learn from but they seem so sluggish while we are going through them. However, we should know that there can't be a testimony without a test, there can't be a story without history, there can't be anything learned without a teaching session. The travel that seems so long is the teaching session, it is the time that we learn the most valuable lessons, and it becomes up to us to take those lessons away from those experiences in order to teach someone else.

This is the lesson in the leading. Luke chapter 4 tells us the story about Jesus as He was led into the wilderness to be tempted by the devil. The Bible records that this leading was immediately after He came off of a forty-day fast. Well, when we come off of fasting, we are to be weak we are expected to want to get nutrients into our body because we have starved ourselves in keeping God's command about denying ourselves. You see the whole message behind fasting is to allow yourself to become one with the spirit and deny the flesh for that period. We deny food to our bodies to open up ourselves to become a channel and conduit that God can speak too and through. So it would seem like a very advantageous time for Satan to come at the Son of God, in order to tempt him. He would be exhausted, He would be prone to taking on any offers that Satan would set before him. So many times, God allows us to be drained or depleted of energy seemingly and then we go through things presented by the enemy. So, the messages that He have instructed us, can be used by us. So that we can capitalize upon what we have been taught. We can successfully divulge the information that God has taught us for the entire time that we were going through. We must also know that as we navigate this life, in our quest to "find me" and also unlock the God-given potential we must be honest with ourselves. If you are like me you probably wondered why does the scripture instructs us that a liar will not tarry in God's sight, why does the scripture warn us so much about the liar? Why does scripture tell us that those who worship Him must worship Him in spirit and in truth? Can it be that the only way to find us is by identifying us? Can it be that as long as we don't be true to ourselves, we can't be truthful with God and consequently we give Him absolutely nothing to work with? Why is it that the scripture implies consequences that would follow the liar? Why is it stressed to be so important? Can't we just develop in our own Godly potential without acknowledging our pains, our short-comings, our faults, our failures, our frailties? Well, I will tell you if that its possible but we just continue to live a miserable existence. I remembered years ago, the spirit instructed me to concentrate on the knowledge that I was a man before I was a minister, meaning that the frailties of my life must be accepted and acknowledged so that I can let God correct them so that I can let and allow God to develop me into the minister that he would like me to be. I like a lot of people in the World, often think about being honest with God and the importance of that and how it would actually give God something to work with. I concluded that it's okay, not to be okay.

If you are like me, you were brought up in the traditional church and the way of thinking that 'we must never question God about the reasons why He has allowed things to be so in our lives' we must accept what God allows. This is true; However, we must also understand the entire complexity of that one statement. God is like our teacher, and we often ask the teacher about things that we don't understand, how to work math problems, how to solve a science equation or algebra even. Well, we must understand that God allows us to come to Him. He is not the quintessential dictator who throws out rules and laws and we just are to bare it and not ask any questions about it. God is not the dictator, in fact He is the sovereign, compassionate and empathic Leader. There is free choice.

However, back to what I was saying about 'it's okay not to be okay.' We can't continue in our quest to find ourselves and capitalize on our God-given potential if we just consistently say we are okay when we are not. I may wake up one morning, not feeling so blessed, not feeling so encouraged, not feeling that life has given me the fair share of anything, and it's okay to be okay with or rather to not be okay with that. I think of the most respectable, modest living Christian who says when asked how they are doing, that they are blessed and highly favored. Well, there are days if you would admit it, that you don't feel so highly favored, not even blessed for that matter. Well, if we can be honest in that inclination we give something for God to work with. Unfortunately, as long as we are not being honest with our feelings then God can't work with our feelings or work on them. I am not okay with what you did! I am not okay with the pandemics and epidemics that we face every day! I don't understand what the plan is for my life right now! It's okay not to be okay. I have questioned several questions and I need answers. If we have these questions that only God can answer then we must go to God.

It's okay not to be okay. Don't get me wrong, we don't ask questions because we don't have a passionate love for God; we ask questions because we want to understand more about the plans of God. Even though we may never understand the total plans of God for our lives, some He will show us. It's okay not to be okay.

Chapter 13
Re-Construction

The bricks may be in ruble right now and all the people can see is the mess, the bricks and the mortar that doesn't look appealing to the mind or the eyes right now. However, if you are like me when I think in retrospect of every area and the times that I looked at my life; I was under construction and tried to fight the process of building. Building in your life may not be grand right now, it may not even feel like the process is worth it, it may not even feel pleasing to the body, but the process must be completed.

We must be willing to make the best out of every situation and every chance we have to get the process finished in our life. Times can be hard when we are in the construction zone, but once we are finished in the construction zone we will appreciate the journey, once we have understood the entire reason that we had to go through the construction in the beginning, we will appreciate it. In this book we will find that in the process of "finding me" or "finding yourself."; requires patience, resilience and perseverance. If you're like me one day you will wake up just to discover that you have spent the majority of your life working on someone else's dream, decorating someone else's house, living vicariously through someone else, looking at the picture through someone else's glasses. You will realize that all the while I was trying to make someone else's life enjoyable, mine was in shambles. The whole time I was acting like the surgeon for someone else's emergency, I didn't get to emerge and see what I could make of my own life. Now where is the time gone, how can I recapture that time that is lost? Can I go and re-live all of that time that was wasted? Can I envision my life as it would have been had I taken the time to invest in my own dreams? My own hopes, my own aspirations? Why did I make the decision to be-labor the issue of fixing someone else's dream, someone else's problem, someone else's potential nightmare? Now I am left with a nightmare of my own. Now I am left to fix a room that is left in shambles, to re-model a house that is swept away and re-modeled by the decorating skills and debacles. Why? Why? Did I let it come to such a past? How did I suffer this infrastructure to become so ruined?

One day I remember it so vividly someone proposed to me the National Voting Rights Acts and they raised the issue that maybe instead of voting for my best candidate I should consider giving myself a vote, I should consider looking at myself in the mirror and telling myself that "I vote for me" "I vote for myself a chance to correct debacles of life." "I vote for myself in order to realize my greatest potential.", "I vote for myself to capitalize and build on those opportunities that I have been given in life to be great." I vote for myself again. I am not going to look at who or what may feel bad about my form of self-care, I am not going to feel bad about who frowns on my form of self-love. I am going to decide to vote for me.

Voting for me sometimes requires that you take courage and build yourself up why do I say this because people are going to be your biggest critics. Yes, they are going to talk about you and how you've found yourself and how now you're interested in yourself, your dreams, your aspirations and yes people will begin to call you things, people will begin to say that you are stuck on yourself, but no that's not it at all, I am concentrating on "finding me". You can't find out what is your God-given potential until you find yourself, until you find you. When you find you, you find what it is that God has designed for you. Because if you are like me you can spend years and years finding your life in someone else's sights and that's not at all what God has designed for you. "For I know the thoughts and plans that I have for you saith the Lord, plans to give you a future and expected end." The key is knowing that His plans are for you, not for the other house that you spent your years decorating but the plans for you. If you are like me you don't like to see the rubble, you don't like to see the stubble that often be-falls most of our lives, but the point in this that sometimes in finding us we have to be exposed to the rubble and to the stubble. We look at the nation and we never thought that the nation would be in such a vulnerable time as this, but it happened and we are to protect ourselves and do what we can do to live through it, cope with the constant obstacles and debacles that life sends our way. We get tired of putting on hand sanitizer, we get tired of having to wear masks where-ever we go, we get tired of having to put on gloves. If you work in the office environment, you get tired of receiving mail and having to let it air out for a couple of days, but sometimes It's necessary to get where we are going. Sometimes the quarantining is necessary for the healing process to begin. With that said we can't find our God Given Potential if we spread the fumes of the construction zone to others. We have to sometimes go into hiding, we have to sometimes let God hide us in the cleft of the rock, because in the cleft of that rock, we find safety and we find assurance that everything that we've ever prayed for will be alright. Everything that we have ever asked God for He has not forgotten and He will answer when we have gotten to a mindset that we can maintain. In our quest to find who we are, we are going to encounter somethings that we rather not deal with, however they will come up again and when that time comes we will have to deal with them. Better sooner than later. Some times in life or in finding ourselves rather we try to skip to the end of the book, we become so thrilled with wanting to know how this whole thing ends up, what the end will look like; however, according to Jeremiah 29:11 we are supposed to know how the end will look, it is the in-between part that we should be seeking God for, asking Him to lead and direct us for it is the middle part that we don't know. We know that everything will work together for our good (Romans 8:28) but it is the part in the middle that we often times can't understand.

Talking to an associate of mine, it was discovered that often times we try to make the middle make sense, I concluded that often times it is not our job to make the middle make sense. It will all make sense at the end of the road. We spend the better part of our lives trying to make something make sense that we were never supposed to help make sense, we were never designed to orchestrate our lives and every adventure that is contained therein. If we were supposed to do so, it would be automatically done, it would magically come together. Unfortunately, life is not majestic, life is not a magical experience; it's a human experience. However, since it is a human experience we can't think we can handle it with a magic wand and make everything that we have ever dealt with make sense. We would literally drive ourselves crazy if we always tried to make sense of every little thing that to us. That's too far to go back. I am too old to count all of the times I have been done wrong or all of the things that I may have said that was taken out of context.

Every time you have been misunderstood to try and add all that up and make some kind of sense out it, or to look back over your whole life and try to make some sort of sense out of it is mundane and trivial at the least. God never wanted us to try to make sense out of the process, He commands us to trust the process, He commands us not to give up in the process. If we give up in the process something inside is not going to be done, something will miss the nutrients that are needed to capitalize on the lessons that we were supposed to learn out of all of it. We can't sit there and try to make sense out of the trials and pitfalls of life, for in doing so how will we ever find ourselves, how will we ever find our God Given Potential.

In construction, we sometimes have to wear a hard hat, steel-toed boots, and other accessories so that we won't end up wounded by the debris and the material that we were trying to build with, so we won't end up getting hit on the head by the very steel we were trying to erect. Most times we are like that in life, we have to put on our PPE so we don't get wounded while the construction worker is trying to build, so we don't become a travesty brought about by our own construction "Collateral Damage" if you will; destroying from the inside out. God desires to see us prosper and be in good health even as our souls would prosper, he doesn't desire to see any of us fall or become wounded as a result of our own construction. He desires to see us whole, walking in the authority that He has given to us. Think it not strange when the fiery darts come to test your faith, for they were meant to come during the construction process, they were meant to come while you're under construction. That's why we wear our PPE, that we may be able to quench every fiery dart of the enemy. Be not alarmed when those who you think you are the closet too will try to bring you down and laugh if they could ever achieve it. "No weapon that is formed against you shall prosper, and every tongue that exalts itself in judgment shall be utterly condemned for this is the heritage of the servants of the Lord and the vindication is of me, saith the Lord." It may form but you can rest assured in the word of God that it will not prosper. God has spoken it and the redemptive work of Jesus on the cross confirms it. Don 't fret because you have that construction hat on your head, don't cry because you have to wear those construction boots right now, don't look down because you have to wear those safety glasses right now. There is a better house that doesn't look anything like the one that we see right now in preparation, there is a better house in construction, there is a stable house on the horizon, there is another house that is waiting to be built; don't mind the mess, I am just under construction.

If you're like me you are asking yourself how do I live in the construction zone? How do I speak when I am in the construction zone? It has been my knowledge that the superintendent just follows the blueprint that has been made. He doesn't know how the house is going to look once he finishes it, he doesn't know if all of the metal is going to meet at the right angle, it is based his ability to follow the blueprint that was drawn. That's why you have to get someone who is trained in blueprint reading to be able to know every acute triangle and isosceles triangle and how they will work together. You can't just be a novice and learn how to live in the construction zone. Let me tell you of a truth, there was a man and his wife in the Bible who was very fair in age, and this couple had no child. It was prophesied that they would have a child, it was told to the father of the child, who was not in belief, looking at the age of his wife and his own age why would He believe it? Why would he even be in expectation of it? It simply wasn't going to happen so he thought. That is one thing that we have got to understand, we may not see all of the provision; however, if there is any vision; God will put the pro on the vision and make "provision". So, in keeping with the story the angel of the Lord knew the importance of John the Baptist, being the forerunner for the promised Messiah and how the birth had to happen and didn't want it to be smeared with any doubt or unbelief, closed Zacharias' mouth until after the birth. So what am I saying to the person who wants to know how to live in the construction zone? I am simply saying "SHUT UP". God can't get the blessing to you sometimes because you won't shut up, you don't know how to behave in the construction zone. The hard hat is to keep out all of the negativity that is just waiting to overtake our minds, the steel-toed boots are there to stop any hard objects from falling and bruising our feet so that we can't walk into the promises of God, our safety goggles are there to keep any dust of other particles from blinding our vision so that we can't see the things of God. We must make sure that we have a clear view of the possibilities that God has for us. For scripture lets us know that God knows the way that we must take, he says that after we have been tried by fire, it is certain that we will come out as pure gold.

Living in the construction zone requires a code of ethics if you will for survival, we can't live in the construction zone if we take everything that people say as an attack on us personally, we can't live in the construction zone if we aren't willing to learn while we are there. We can't live in the construction zone if we are unable to build off of criticisms that may come to make us better. We can't live in the construction zone if we consistently see us alone and ignore the fact that there is a world around us. Many people live and ignore the fact that God blesses us to be a blessing to others, and we can't identify those to bless if we are consistently focused on ourselves. God wants us to know that being a conduit for blessings to flow through is part of construction zone living. Many people don't want to be labeled as being in a construction zone. However, the construction zone is where we are made, the construction zone is where we get fuel to make it to the next season in our lives and if we fail in the process of living in the construction zone, how will we ever get to the next season. The next season is predicated on how we survive in construction zone living.

Having your feet shod with the preparation of the gospel of peace is another thing that we have to have when living in the construction zone. We must wear the part of the PPE and that is our protective boots, we must have our steel toes on so we can be able to walk into the blessings that God has for us. Without those boots, steel may drop on our toes, anything that may cause our foot to become broken so that we may not be able to walk into the season that God is arranging for us. We may have many types of boots that we can wear, it just matters that our boots are those steel-toe boots, they are those boots that will help us navigate through the hard-falling metal that is coming in our lives to cause us to stumble or cause us to fall.

Zacharias had a muzzle put on by the angel of the Lord for his construction zone. Although not a piece of PPE it is needed to most oftentimes, sometimes we can become the greatest hindrance to our blessing by not shutting or mouths. When the scripture instructs us to be still and know that I am God. It instructs us to do just that, be still. That means that we can't say nothing, that we shouldn't say nothing, it's not that we can't but it is that we shouldn't. The process for fulfillment is not yet ready. This is why the angel gave Zacharias' mouth a restraining order. This restraining order warranted him not to speak until the birth of the child, well the angel made it where he couldn't talk.

Fortunately, we know that in today's society there is not going to be an angel that takes our ability to speak away, so it becomes incumbent upon us not to let negativity come out of our gateways and that is our mouths. God does not make it where we are not allowed to speak, He just commissions us to believe and not speak negativity into our situation. God is for us and not against us. It is only through our negativity are the ill feelings birthed, through our negativity is depravity recognized, through our negativity are dreams unfulfilled and not realized. If we can just learn how to shut up in the valleys, we can know how to praise on the mountaintop.

Right here reminds me of one of the sub-titles of an earlier passage, the sub-title was listening to the elevator music. If you're like me, you ask what's going on with all of this elevator music? Does it actually have a point? And if there is a point is there actually an end? What is it for? Who does it entertain? Is it even there to entertain? Why was it placed there? If it serves no real purpose, why is it even there? Is it just placed there for me to aimlessly listen to? Knowing that there is really no significant purpose that it has or even serves? It's just elevator music; it's just there often to distract you, it's just there often to get you frustrated and want to throw in the per-verbial towel of life and say "I quit." We all get in that rut of life where we are forced to listen to the elevator music but my friends that's just what it is: "elevator music"; it serves no purpose at all. It is just there to distract you, often times serving as a conduit of transportation to get you from one mode to another. Let the elevator music play. It's there to distract you, don't lose Focus on you. Don't lose Focus on what you are supposed to be doing. Sooner or later that track is going to run out. Sometimes we all find ourselves in the wondering stage of life, wondering where am I going? When will I get there? How fast is this thing called life is going to take to get me there? Well let me inform you that it is not up for us to find out. It is up to us to trust the one who created us, the one who is directing our steps. Job stated, "Behold I go forward, but he is not there; and backward, but I cannot perceive him: On the left hand, where he doth work, but I cannot behold him: he hideth himself on the right hand, that I cannot see him: But he knoweth the way that I take: when he hath tried me, I shall come out as pure gold"(Job 23:8-10). We must trust him even if we can't trace him. The festival of the new moon in the Hebrew culture in Colossians 2:16-17 had a great message for Israel as it was the appointed time for of His choosing to reveal or give the prophetic revelation to His people of His purposes for them. However, now in modern we have to trust Him until He chooses to reveal His plans for us. Fortunately, there is good news, and the news is that He knows the plans and thoughts that He thinks towards us for they are good and not evil plans to give us a future and hope (Jer. 29:11). Sometimes we become so frustrated because of our inability to figure out the plan, we shiver and want to get all the way out of the plan. However, in the quest to find me, we must trust the divinity of our God to find us, and the real us is the one that He created us to be. If God gave us the entire pieces to our puzzle in life, we wouldn't know what to do with it. So we find out in part, we find out as we go, and we trust Him for the rest.

Chapter 14
Renewal of your Focus

I once heard someone tell me that ocus is the Seed for Uncommon Productivity. Sometimes in life things come to get us out of line, to deter our Focus, cause a detour in our road to success. If we allow it sometimes it will grip the very fibers of our being and lead us down a road that will just end in tragedy. However, we are to look again, look again! Renew your Focus put on your glasses, use the eyes behind the eyes and become uncommon. God has created us to be uncommon in this common world, He has called us to be supernatural in this natural world and sometimes circumstances cause us to lose that focus, however just like I said earlier focus is the seed for uncommon productivity.

I had a conversation with a brother, and we talked about the desire of people to know what the whole picture entails. We talked and concluded that God will never give you the whole picture, He designs the picture of the future and you decide it. Saying you decide it, you decide whether you are going to trust Him with it enough to praise Him in the meantime while you are waiting on the blessing. Decide to be a praiser and worshipper even though the pieces of the puzzle hadn't come together yet, praise Him even when you can't focus everything in your life is a blur, praise Him even when you are crying on the inside, praise Him even when repossessions occur, praise Him when she walks out or when He walks out. Trusting the process that is what we call it. God refines us in the process. If you are like me, you can identify with being antsy, you can identify with wanting to know, it's not for you to know. I've found that in this life sometimes, more often than not, we have re-discover, re-invent, re-look, re-try and even re-focus. The whole plan of the enemy is to make us lose focus on the original plan, the original blueprint, the original road map. Glory be to God, that we have a default drive, computers are not the only things that have a default drive. A default drive is a drive that takes us back to the original algorithm in computers, it takes us back to the start or how the program was originally supposed to be. We may find ourselves in broken marriages, broken homes, broken careers things that are just broken. However, if we can manage to make it to the default drive, if we can manage to turn off everything that may have us dealing with the failures in our lives and look to the original program. Sometimes we have to go back to COBOL the beginning computer language, sometimes we have to go back to the Dot Matrix Printer, which is the original cycle of life, so to speak. I know I am using computer terminology, but I'm using this a metaphor to show you that you can do this in your life.

The prodigal son, we know the story he asked his father to give him all of the money that was coming to him as being a son so that he could go out and make it on his own. The Bible records that he went out and after time he spent all of his money on riotous living, he spent until he had no more. It is funny how in times of plenty you have friends, but in times of famine your friends become obsolete. The story goes on to let us know that he spent all of his money on riotous living, and he came to a begging place a vulnerable state. Most of the time we don't fit in this same scenario but we have spent all we have emotionally. We got into that marriage that caused us to use all of what we had emotionally and it left us mentally drained, broke, busted and like the term goes disgust. We are left to re-discover ourselves again, because we lost ourselves in the turmoil and the repetition of trying to fit when it doesn't work. He had to find himself, the scripture records that he began to eat with the pigs and that was the turning point of the story, there he remembered that he had much better times at his father's house, there he didn't have to eat with the pigs, there he didn't have to think about where he was going to lay his head, there he didn't have to think about what he was going to eat the next day. He came to himself. You see, there is power in remembering, just like it can be a curse, it can also become a blessing as well, it is what we choose to remember, it is the good things or the bad things. He rebooted, he used the default drive. He went back home. The Bible records that when the father saw him coming from a far off, he recognized him. We think most of the time that God has forgotten what we look like, but God still recognizes us, He still knows exactly what we walk like, He knows whether we have a limp or a slew-foot. He knows exactly how we swing our arms when we walk. God is able to recognize us.

His father recognized him, and stated that my son who was lost and now found had come back home, the scripture records that he prepared the fattest calf and called for a ring to be placed on his hand to start a celebration because his son who was lost has now come back home. Re-boot and go back home, find your default drive and go back home.

We sometimes think that we can't go back home. Sometime we think that God will not remember us and that what has happened in our lives is too bad or too uncomfortable for us to even come back home. There is always room to come back. We can always find me. Finding me is not what you think; finding me is finding what and who God created you to be, discovering your God-given potential.

Many of us had experiences where we lost us, we lost ourselves, we lost the ability to focus on the picture that God created and set before us. He must focus and get the re-vamping of the picture that was originally set before us. Sometimes we get so caught up in making money, and sometimes we get so caught up in trying to be well off, that we forget or even forfeit the plan that God had for us. The reason why I say forfeit, sometimes we don't remember to come back or either the devil and the adversary catches us on the outside of the will of God. If you are like me, you have had experiences in life that have come to cause you forcefully to lose who you are, to cause you to tread a different road than what was originally the plan for you. However, there is a God that gives us what we need to get back in the saddle. Trials and pitfalls try to make you forget what He has done thus far, getting caught up with the cares of life trying to make money, trying to change your status in life, trying to change the narrative of life. We need to know that God makes the narrative; God writes and re-writes the story if we allow Him to do so.

Acceptance is what causes us to change the narrative of our lives, we have to accept the fact that we lost us, we lost ourselves. When we learn to accept the picture that we created by following the cares of life, God can better implement the changing of the narrative. When we realize and be truthful with ourselves about what we were a part of wasn't really us, it didn't really fit then we are welcomed to move on with our lives. Sometimes we want so eagerly to fit into a life that wasn't meant for us to be a part of, we discover that sometimes it is in fact our desire to make that aspect a part of our story that we fail to realize that it subtracted and never would've adequately added to our story.

Made in the USA
Columbia, SC
01 October 2024